THE LOST SHIPS OF
GUADALCANAL

THE LOST SHIPS OF
GUADALCANAL

BY ROBERT D. BALLARD

WITH RICK ARCHBOLD

Contemporary photographs
by Michael McCoy
Underwater paintings by Ken Marschall
Technical and Historical consultation
by Richard B. Frank
and Charles Haberlein, Jr.

A VIKING / MADISON PRESS BOOK

First published in Canada by
Penguin Books Canada Limited
10 Alcorn Avenue, Toronto, Ontario M4V 3B2

Canadian Cataloguing in Publication Data

Ballard, Robert D.
The lost ships of Guadalcanal

Includes index.
ISBN 0-670-85292-9

1. Shipwrecks - Iron Bottom Sound. 2. Guadalcanal Island (Solomon Islands), Battle of, 1942-1943.
I. Archbold, Rick, 1950- . II. Marschall, Ken. III. Title.

D767.98.B34 1993   940.54'26   C93-094022-9

Produced by
Madison Press Books
40 Madison Avenue
Toronto, Ontario
Canada M5R 2S1

Printed in Italy

(Page 1) *The First Marine Division crest proudly displays the unit's greatest victory, Guadalcanal, along with the stars of the Southern Cross.*

(Pages 2-3) *Surf breaks over war wreckage on a Guadalcanal beach.*

(Below) *Under puffs of anti-aircraft fire, an American destroyer races across Iron Bottom Sound on invasion day, August 7, 1942.*

(Pages 6-7) *The submarine* Sea Cliff *illuminates an anemone-encrusted gun on the sunken Australian cruiser* Canberra.

(Page 8-9) *American war artist Dwight Shepler painted this watercolor of artillery lookouts on Guadalcanal's Bloody Knoll in 1942.*

CONTENTS

For Chester P. Ballard, Harry W. Earle, Jr., John A. Earle,
and William H. Earle, who spent the war years in harm's way, and for the men
and women who participated in the historic events of World War II.

CHAPTER ONE

GUADALCANAL RETURN

July 25, 1992

AS THE PLANE BANKED, I STARED OUT THE WINDOW at an idyllic vista of sparkling blue water and rugged green islands rimmed with white beaches and coral reefs. It made me think of the mystical land of Bali Hai in the musical *South Pacific*, a place to forget one's cares and troubles.

One does not come to Guadalcanal to forget, however, but to remember. For here was waged one of the epic struggles of World War II, when the whole course of the Pacific conflict seemed to hang in the balance. As I stared out the window I imagined I could see beneath the water's beguiling surface to the battlefield graveyard below, the last resting place of the nearly fifty ships that

(Left) Cape Esperance on western Guadalcanal, where the Japanese landed many of their troops. (Above) An American tank left to rust in Guadalcanal's jungle.

gave these waters their name: Iron Bottom Sound. They were my reason for being on this flight from Fiji to Henderson Field, Guadalcanal, Solomon Islands. The lost ships of Guadalcanal.

Guadalcanal quickly loses some of its postcard prettiness when you know its wartime history. In 1942 Iron Bottom Sound was a twin-jawed trap for Japanese and Allied ships. The jaws of the trap face west, where wild, sparsely populated Savo Island stands sentinel over the sound's two most navigable approaches—the inevitable routes of attack. Savo's distinctive volcanic contour was the unmistakable shape that the Japanese, American and Australian sailors who fought in these waters recalled most vividly, especially the way she looked emerging from a rain squall or bathed in silver moonlight. Around her skirts some of the bloodiest and most pivotal naval battles of the Pacific war were fought, almost always by night.

When I first began thinking about Guadalcanal and the ships sunk in nearby waters, I knew only vaguely of the momentous events that happened there. As a boy growing up in the navy town of San Diego, California, just after the war, I'd heard many tales of the great battles in the Pacific, Guadalcanal prominent among them. But most of my boyhood images of Guadalcanal came from movies and television—especially from the TV documentary series I devoured, *Victory at Sea* in particular. I can still hear Richard Rodgers' stirring theme music for that patriotic celebration of American military prowess. These programs—along with *Baa, Baa Black Sheep*, a later television series starring Robert Conrad as a daring fighter pilot—made Guadalcanal seem like a battle fought primarily on land and in the air. Ships and sailors were seldom if ever seen (except unloading more troops to fight the nasty Nipponese in the stinking jungle). Yet in fact more Americans died in Guadalcanal waters than on land.

For all the fame of its air and land battles,

RICHARD TREGASKIS' **GUADALCANAL DIARY**

DIRECTED BY
LEWIS SEILER
PRODUCED BY
BRYAN FOY
ASSOCIATE PRODUCER
ISLIN AUSTER
SCREEN PLAY BY
LAMAR TROTTI
ADAPTATION BY
JERRY CADY

PRESTON **FOSTER**
LLOYD **NOLAN**
WILLIAM **BENDIX**
RICHARD **CONTE**
ANTHONY **QUINN**

A 20th CENTURY-FOX *Encore Hit!*

(Opposite) Guadalcanal's mountains appear through the clouds. (Above and left) Through books and movies, Guadalcanal became one of the most documented battles of the Second World War.

Guadalcanal is at least as compelling a story of sailors and warships, of admirals both rash and timid, of acts of individual heroism and compassion, of the terrifying confusion of a night naval action, of the unparalleled horror of being trapped in a stricken burning ship. It is one of the great naval stories of any war.

As our plane leveled off and began its descent I squeezed my wife's hand. Like countless Americans and Japanese, Barbara felt a personal link to this deceptively pretty tropical island. Her uncle, John Earle, was an army air force operations officer stationed at Henderson Field later in the war, after it had become a secure staging point for the Allied offensive. In January 1944, the plane taking him to New Zealand for some well-earned leave disappeared. For many months his young wife, Celine, refused to believe he was dead, but he was never heard from again.

Whether or not you had a relative or a friend who fought there, Guadalcanal conjures up all the horror—

and the glory — of the Pacific war and was, according to many historians, its most crucial episode. Pearl Harbor was a shocking defeat for the Americans, but in retrospect seems a colossal strategic blunder by the Japanese, since it brought the United States into the war earlier and with greater emotional commitment than might otherwise have been the case. The Battle of Midway in early June of 1942 was the first clearcut U.S. victory, and a stunning one at that, coming against a superior Japanese force at a time when the emperor's legions seemed unstoppable. (The Japanese lost four aircraft carriers and 225 airplanes; the Americans one carrier and 150 aircraft.) But it was at Guadalcanal that the two giants first went toe to toe, belly to belly, in a titanic slugfest that ultimately proved to be the Pacific war's true turning point. There were no successful Japanese offensives in the Pacific after Guadalcanal and no more American retreats. The fall of Guadalcanal opened the gateway to Tokyo. Had the Japanese won this crucial round, there's no telling how much longer the war would have taken or how many more lives on both sides it would have cost.

It all began with an airfield—the same airfield toward which our plane was now rapidly descending. Despite the defeat at Midway, the Japanese remained supremely confident. In the first six months of the war they had conquered a vast area including French Indochina, the Philippines and the Dutch East Indies. Now they were eyeing Papua, the Australian-controlled part of New Guinea, and perhaps even Australia itself. Guadalcanal, a previously unimportant island in the recently occupied British Solomon Islands Protectorate, was the farthest southeastward extension of Japanese power in the Pacific. In late June 1942, Japanese construction troops and heavy equipment landed on the island's north coast near a place called Lunga Point and began building an airstrip. When complete, this would serve as an advance base that would cover the western flank of the thrust southeast through Papua and threaten U.S. bases as far away as New Caledonia.

When the Americans learned what the Japanese were up to, their plans to use the eastern Solomons as the first stage of their first offensive of the Pacific war took on an extra edge. This operation, code-named Watchtower, was the brainchild of the abrasive Commander in Chief of the United States Fleet and Chief of Naval Operations, Admiral Ernest J. King,

THE LOST SHIPS OF GUADALCANAL

(Left) Today Henderson Field is the airport for Honiara, the capital of the Solomons. (Right) Fifty years ago, it was dominated by "the Pagoda," a Japanese building that later served as the American headquarters. (Below) A modern jet passes in front of the wartime control tower.

come, its airfield would become a chess piece over which two great military powers would fight at incredible cost. The longer the contest and the greater the resources expended by each side, the more significant this prize became. It may have started out as a pawn, but it ended up as the king.

Guadalcanal was also a deadly dress rehearsal for the island-hopping American offensive to come. Here the United States learned to fight a new kind of war, one that involved the complex coordination of ships, planes and land troops in sometimes nightmarish conditions. To the sailors sealed inside sweltering ships, to the pilots who bailed out of burning fighters only to spend days adrift in shark-infested waters facing sunstroke and starvation, to the soldiers fighting hand to hand in steaming malarial jungles, this was definitely war as hell. It was made more hellish by the dreadful strategic mistakes and terrible tactical decisions on both sides; both the Japanese and the Americans suffered humiliating defeats and marred victories. The thing that really astonished me as I came to know the story of Guadalcanal in more detail was what a beating the American side took—the fabled marines and the proud navy—and how often the U. S. was on the ropes, close to losing everything.

Nonetheless the United States did hang on, and did drive the Japanese from Guadalcanal. And it was the navy that ultimately made this possible, even if at times the marines on the island felt as though the admirals had abandoned them to starve or be massacred in a godforsaken place. The naval story of Guadalcanal is not dominated by a single ship or a single battle. It is the story of a series of battles and skirmishes strung out over a period of months. Two of these battles stand out above all others. The first was fought on the night of August 8-9, 1942, and ranks as the most humiliating defeat ever suffered by the American navy. A fleet that should have been ready to fight was caught divided and napping by an inferior attacker who escaped virtually unscathed while sinking four heavy cruisers. It was a long time before the folks back home were told the true extent of the Allied defeat at what has come to be known as the Battle of Savo Island, and military historians are still apportioning the blame.

Savo Island was a costly blow to American naval pride, but not strategically decisive. The later Naval Battle of Guadalcanal—really a series of engagements, including two major night battles, fought from

who was determined to go on the attack as soon as possible. King saw the capture of Guadalcanal as the first step in the reconquest of Japan's Pacific gains. According to his grand plan, it would provide the staging point for an Allied advance up the Solomon Islands chain into the Bismarck Archipelago and ultimately to the potent Japanese base at Rabaul, New Britain. News of the Japanese airstrip simply made his plan more urgent. It must be seized before enemy airplanes could land there. The air base must become American, not Japanese.

And so, in late July an Allied armada assembled south of Fiji and set sail for an island few of its participants had ever heard of. In the six months of fighting to

(Above) After Guadalcanal was won, American ships would show their respect for the fallen by making "S" turns when sailing across Iron Bottom Sound. (Left) The now-tranquil waters off Savo Island. (Opposite) The rusting remains of battle on a tropical beach.

November 12 to November 15, 1942—was the watershed. By this time American forces on Guadalcanal had survived, but barely, three determined Japanese offensives and were bracing themselves for a fourth, which seemed sure to be the most powerful of all. The first night battle, fought in the early hours of November 13, was a chaotic brawl more like a battle from the days of sail than a modern naval engagement. Before it was over, two American admirals had lost their lives and a Japanese admiral had lost both his flagship and his reputation. The second night battle, fought on the night of November 14-15, featured one of the last of the few surface actions between those soon-to-be-obsolete nautical dinosaurs,

battleships, the floating gun platforms that most prewar strategists believed would be the decisive weapons of modern naval warfare. In the Naval Battle of Guadalcanal, both sides suffered heavily. But the Japanese attempt to reinforce their troops on the island was largely thwarted, their fleet and their resolve weakened. In the end, this series of sea battles proved to be the critical episode in the six-month struggle.

Given this complex history, I knew Guadalcanal was going to be unlike any expedition I had previously mounted. I was looking not for a single ship but for many ships. I was exploring not a single wreck but an entire battlefield. The challenge for my team would be not

simply to find several ships, but to find both Japanese and Allied ships that related to the most important parts of the story.

As our plane's landing gear lowered, I contemplated the task that lay ahead. A little less than a year ago, in the fall of 1991, our preliminary expedition had located ten wrecks in Iron Bottom Sound. Working on a minimal budget and with only a primitive sonar, we weren't able to positively identify all the ships we had discovered. Now, thanks to the support of the U.S. Navy, we were returning with two top-of-the line pieces of equipment—the submersible *Sea Cliff* (a brother of the *Alvin* sub in which I dove on the *Titanic*) and *Scorpio* (a close cousin of *Jason*, the remotely operated camera vehicle I had developed for deep sea exploration). With *Sea Cliff*

and *Scorpio* we hoped to be able to bring back superb still and video pictures of the wrecks—if we had found ships representing each phase of the major battles or could find them in the short time available.

As we began our final descent I could see the gentle outline of Bloody Ridge, where in mid-September 1942 the marines had somehow held off the first major Japanese attack—and the one that came closest to succeeding. Last year I'd walked the ridge and been shocked by the tacky American monument to the brave young men who had died there; it was in startling and painful contrast to the gleaming Japanese memorial. This year—the fiftieth anniversary of the landings was less than two weeks away—the United States would rectify this state of affairs by dedicating a new memorial to all the

(Opposite, top and above) The remnants of war are everywhere in the Solomon Islands. (Below) The modern Australian warship Canberra approaches Savo Island, in waters where her namesake was sunk more than fifty years ago.

soldiers, sailors and airmen who perished. For this and the attendant celebrations, hundreds of veterans had decided to return to the place the Japanese nicknamed Starvation Island and the Americans simply called the Canal. Two of these men were on this flight, returning for the first time in fifty years.

I'd spoken to them briefly when our plane took off from Fiji several hours before. They had been polite and friendly, betraying no hint of the complex emotions they must have been feeling. Dr. James Cashman had been the medical officer on board the destroyer *Cushing* when it sank on the night of November 13 during the first phase of the Naval Battle of Guadalcanal. (At over six feet and two hundred pounds, the former college football lineman must have found the quarters cramped on the small destroyer.) An enemy shell killed most of those in the wardroom where he was tending the wounded. He survived with a few scratches and kept on working until the captain ordered abandon ship. Stewart Moredock, now a retired professor of mathematics, had been Rear Admiral Norman Scott's young operations officer aboard *Atlanta* during the first night of the Naval Battle of Guadalcanal. Moredock was standing a few feet away from Scott when the admiral took his last step. For most of the past fifty years he had blotted out that memory. Now both Cashman and Moredock were returning to bury the demons and, we all hoped, to look again on their former ships.

Arriving on other flights were two other naval survivors: Bert Warne, who had been a seaman on the Australian heavy cruiser *Canberra* sunk at Savo Island, and Michiharu Shinya, the torpedo officer on the Japanese destroyer *Akatsuki*, sunk on November 13. (Shinya was captured and spent the remainder of the war as a POW in New Zealand.)

As the plane hit the tarmac and taxied to the terminal, I tried to imagine myself inside the skins of Cashman and Moredock. Were they regretting the decision to return to this place of nightmares? Were they already beginning to relive long-buried events? But it was time to grab hand luggage and disembark. As Barbara and I emerged from the airplane hatchway, we were punched by a hot fist of humid air, which instantly fused the modern Guadalcanal and the historical one. This was the place of which an unknown lyricist wrote, "Say a prayer for your pal / on Guadalcanal. / He needs God's help, it's true."

THE JAPANESE ADVANCE

*By August 1942
Japan had reached the
apex of its power.*

The Japanese attack on Pearl Harbor was just one in a series of lightning opening moves that caught the Allies off-guard.

Even Japan's own military planners were astonished at the speed and ease of her initial conquests. Immediately following the attack on Pearl Harbor, her forces moved on multiple fronts in southeast Asia and the southwestern Pacific. Despite ample warning, General MacArthur was caught napping at Manila and his air force was destroyed on the ground, leaving the Philippines indefensible. In mid-February the supposedly impregnable British fortress of Singapore and its nearly 140,000 service personnel fell in what one historian has called "the greatest military defeat in all British history."

Meanwhile Allied naval forces (Dutch, American, British) offered ineffectual resistance as amphibious Japanese legions gobbled up the Dutch East Indies and secured the oil resources their country so desperately needed. The Allies' last stand at the Battle of the Java Sea in late February was a complete rout and by March 1942 Japan's dream of conquest was almost a reality, a self-sufficient Greater East Asia Co-Prosperity Sphere that comprised all the southeast Asian and western Pacific possessions of France, the Netherlands and Great Britain. Instead of stopping to consolidate her gains, however, Japan now pushed further, succumbing to what one of her own admirals later called "victory disease." Emperor Hirohito sagely commented at the time, "the fruits of victory are tumbling into our mouths too quickly."

(Above) The Emperor's troops come ashore in the Dutch East Indies. This followed the Japanese sweep down the Malay peninsula and the fall of Singapore (below), once Britain's "Invincible Fortress."

ZENITH OF THE RISING SUN

By August 7, 1942, the Japanese Empire stretched from Burma in the west across the Pacific to Alaska's Aleutian Islands. Stunned by their own success, the Japanese were desperately trying to consolidate their gains. The airfield under construction on Guadalcanal represented the extreme southeastern outpost of their Empire.

(Left) In Burma, the Japanese were pressing on toward India. (Right, top and bottom) Japanese losses during June 1942's Battle of Midway represented a serious setback, as satirized in the cartoon on the opposite page drawn by a marine artist.

PARADISE LOST

The Solomon Islanders found themselves caught up in a world struggle.

A s of May 3, 1942, when Japanese troops landed on Tulagi, the eastern Solomons effectively joined the Greater East Asia Co-Prosperity Sphere. The newly subject peoples were almost entirely the Melanesians who had inhabited this remote corner of the Pacific since long before an explorer named

(Right) Japanese troops landing at Buka Island in the northwest Solomons, on March 8, 1942.

Don Alvaro Mendaño had bumped into the archipelago in 1567 and claimed it for Spain. The Melanesians lived much as they always had, in isolated and fiercely independent villages, speaking distinct dialects, and subsisting on fishing, hunting and simple agriculture.

The Japanese made little effort to win over the locals through diplomacy. Instead they simply ordered co-operation and threatened punishment. On Guadalcanal, co-operation meant helping build the airstrip. Since the conquerors did not offer to pay for this labor, most of the Melanesians chose not to volunteer. Some gathered intelligence for the coastwatchers, but the majority simply waited to see which way the winds of war would blow.

(Above) The Solomon Islands stretched more than 500 miles from Rabaul in the northwest to San Cristobal, southeast of Guadalcanal, and comprised a disparate group of islands whose people spoke hundreds of different languages and dialects. (Right) Japanese troops teach propaganda songs in a village near Rabaul.

For most people in the South Seas the issues the war was fought over were, at first, quite distant. These children in New Guinea (left) standing in line to greet the Japanese look more apprehensive than frightened. (Right) Soon the people of Japan's conquests were put to work for the benefit of their new Imperial masters.

THE LUCKY LANDING

August 7, 1942

QUARTERMASTER SECOND CLASS THOMAS MORRIS made a pencil note in the quartermaster's log, then stared once again through the pilothouse windows into the predawn darkness of August 7, 1942. The rain and cloud that had cloaked the Allied armada for most of the previous twenty-four hours had now withdrawn to reveal a quarter moon rising to the northeast.

Not for the first time since joining the heavy cruiser U.S.S. *Quincy*, Morris reflected on just how far he had traveled from home and hearth—the family dairy farm in upstate New York that was the only world he had known prior to joining the navy. Before enlisting he had never spent a night in a strange bed. By his own admission, when he arrived on board fresh from quartermaster school he still had "manure between his toes." But now, nearly a year later and at the ripe old age of twenty-two, he was a proud part of a floating fighting machine of more than eleven hundred men.

And *Quincy* was but one small part of the greatest gathering of Allied ships yet seen in the Pacific. The total

(Below) A painting by war artist Dwight Shepler shows Tulagi harbor after the invasion.

expeditionary force for Operation Watchtower comprised more than eighty vessels and included three aircraft carriers, one battleship, eleven heavy cruisers and three light cruisers, thirty-six destroyers and twenty-two transports carrying roughly 19,000 troops of the First and Fifth Marine regiments. The overall commander of the expedition was Vice Admiral Frank Jack Fletcher aboard the aircraft carrier *Saratoga*, which with the two other carriers had taken up position south of Guadalcanal and would provide air support. In direct command of the amphibious landing force was Rear Admiral Richmond Kelly Turner (known as Terrible Turner because of his volcanic temper) who had until recently held down a desk job in Washington. *Quincy*'s job, along with the

other warships now about to enter the sound north of the island of Guadalcanal, was to soften up the island's shore defenses, then provide cover for the troops as they stormed ashore.

"New course, heading 090." Captain Samuel Moore's voice was low but firm. As *Quincy*'s helmsman spun the wheel and the ship heeled sharply to port, the mood on the darkened bridge became even more tense and expectant. Those who spoke did so in hushed tones. Captain Moore—an Annapolis man who was well liked by both officers and crew—walked outside the pilothouse onto the starboard bridge wing for a better look as *Quincy* turned east toward the brightening sky. A few moments later, Morris had to shield his eyes against the first rays

(Left) A rare color shot of Quincy off Fiji, a few days before the invasion. (Above) Thomas Morris, wearing his winter cap with its Quincy band. (Below) Quincy's commanding officer, Captain Samuel Moore.

of the rising sun. Before him was a lovely mountainous green island, something off a travel poster. An unlikely spot for a battle, he thought, but surely somewhere under those palm trees lurked Japanese soldiers and Japanese guns. Now he waited, as did men on the bridges of the other Allied ships, both American and Australian, for the enemy salvo that would surely greet their arrival.

But the first shot came from *Quincy*, which led the line of ships now entering the channel between Cape Esperance, the island's northwestern promontory, and Savo. Almost immediately, her 8-inch guns were joined by others as salvo after salvo raked Lunga Point, the coastal area just north of the Japanese airfield, where it was assumed the enemy's defensive batteries were positioned. Their fire was not returned. Was it possible that the Japanese had been caught napping?

The invasion force now divided in two. One group, which included the Australian heavy cruiser *Canberra*, headed northeast for the small island of Tulagi nestled just under Florida (the island that formed the northeastern boundary of the sound). Meanwhile the larger prong, with *Quincy* in the van, took up a position off a beach east of Lunga Point—code-named Beach Red—which was the designated landing point for the main assault. The marine commander, Major General A. Archer Vandegrift, expected to find five thousand Japanese on the island, including over two thousand infantry. He anticipated that this, the first major amphibious assault by United States armed forces since the Spanish-American War of the 1890s, would be a costly one.

At 0910 the first wave of marines clambered over the sides of their Higgins landing craft and splashed ashore. There was still no sign of resistance as the first troops advanced inland, but the dense Guadalcanal jungle soon slowed them down. Scores of Higgins boats shuttled back and forth between the transports and the beach as spotter airplanes from the cruisers flew overhead. Soon the scene on the beach verged on chaos as the boats, which were now ferrying equipment and supplies ashore, piled up at the beachhead. They simply couldn't be unloaded fast enough. Otherwise the operation seemed to be off to a brilliant start.

But appearances can be deceiving. America was not yet fully ready for a major offensive in the Pacific. Despite the heady U.S. victory at Midway, the fleet was still recovering from its losses at Pearl Harbor nine months earlier. And Roosevelt's Europe First policy meant that the bulk of U.S. troops and weapons were committed to the upcoming invasion of North Africa. The green marines now landing on Guadalcanal and Tulagi had been slated for several months more training before seeing any action. And there was serious question as to whether the troops could be kept adequately armed and resupplied once they were ashore. Before long Operation Watchtower would earn the nickname Operation Shoestring.

Luckily for the Americans, the Guadalcanal landings seem to have caught the Japanese almost totally by surprise. They were preoccupied with their own invasion of Papua, which had begun on July 21 when 16,000 soldiers landed near Buna on New Guinea's northeastern coast and began the difficult advance over the Owen Stanley Mountain range toward Port Moresby. Although the Guadalcanal airstrip was nearly complete, no planes had yet been earmarked for it. In fact, the vast territory Japan now controlled stretched her resources to the limit. And she could not believe the Americans would go on the offensive so soon after Pearl Harbor.

W ORD OF THE INVASION QUICKLY REACHED THE nearest Japanese base at Rabaul, 565 miles northwest of Guadalcanal. Early that morning at Vunakanau Airfield, Petty Officer First Class Saburo Sakai and the other pilots of the combat-hardened Tainan Air Group were just strapping themselves into the cockpits of their Zero long-range fighters, when excited orderlies ran up shouting that their flight had been canceled. First irritated, then curious, the fliers hurriedly returned to the command post for new instructions. There, an angry commander, Tadashi Nakajima, brusquely confirmed that the mission to attack the Allied fighter base at Rabi near the eastern tip of New Guinea was off. Only a few hours earlier a powerful enemy invasion force had attacked the islands of Guadalcanal and nearby Tulagi. The last radio message from the Tulagi garrison had come at 0805: "We pray for the enduring fortunes of war" and pledge to fight "to the last man." Sakai's best friend Lieutenant Junichi Sasai looked sick at the news. His sister's husband, a flying-boat commander, was stationed at Tulagi. He had no doubt his brother-in-law was already dead.

Shock and anger turned into incredulity when Nakajima curtly announced, "You are going to fly the longest fighter operation in history." Their new target was nearly 600 miles away. This was no problem for the Betty attack planes, but it was at the limit of the Zeros' operational range and well outside what the Val dive bombers could manage. Those that couldn't make it back to Rabaul were to head either for a rough airstrip at Buka off the northern point of Bougainville or for a ditching point near Shortland Island off Bougainville's southern end, where a flying boat would be waiting to pick up the pilots. The planes would simply have to be sacrificed.

Shortly after 0930 all the planes were airborne: twenty-seven twin-engined Bettys with eighteen Zeros as escorts and nine unescorted Vals. Sakai, a poor orphan of proud Samurai ancestry, noted with annoyance that the Bettys had not taken time to switch from bombs to torpedoes, which were far more effective against shipping. But he was excited at the prospect of taking on U.S. Navy fliers and airplanes, reputed to be the best the Americans had.

The Zeros reached 13,000 feet, then leveled off heading east over sparkling blue water and lush green tropical islands. After turning south at Buka, the northwestern tip of Bougainville, the hot sun coming in through the cockpit canopy made Sakai thirsty, so he slit the cork in a bottle of soda pop, forgetting the effect of low pressure on a carbonated beverage. In seconds the sticky liquid was all over the cockpit and, though it dried quickly, it left his goggles completed coated. Flying almost blind, his fighter wandering crazily within the formation, he eventually cleaned off the lenses. But it was hardly an auspicious start to the mission.

This air sortie was the first but not the only Japanese response to the Allied invasion. As soon as he received word of the landings, Vice Admiral Gunichi Mikawa, commander of the Japanese Eighth Fleet based at Rabaul, made plans for a night counterattack and quickly assembled all the naval forces available to him. These comprised five heavy cruisers, two light cruisers and one aging destroyer. It was not a well-balanced team and had never maneuvered together before, but there was no alternative. Mikawa knew neither how many nor how heavy were the ships he would be facing, but he soon realized that a swift response held the greatest hope of disrupting and perhaps defeating the enemy.

*(Right) Japanese ace Saburo
Sakai, and (above) a flight
of Zero fighters. A fast,
maneuverable aircraft
capable of operating either
from land (below) or from
aircraft carriers (bottom),
the Zero was a match for any
Allied fighter then flying.*

*Tulagi, the pre-war center of British rule in the Solomons, showing the effects of the Allied bombardment.
The Japanese had chosen to install the bulk of their defensive troops here and not on Guadalcanal.*

COMPARED TO THE CLAUSTROPHOBIC HEAT OF THE *Canberra*'s after engine room, where temperatures often exceeded one hundred degrees Fahrenheit, Stoker Second Class George Faulkner found the humid tropical breeze almost as refreshing as a long, cold draft of beer. He and his fellow "debonair dustmen," as the engine and boiler room crews were nicknamed, had been down below throughout the opening phases of the landings. Now, in late morning, he was getting his first look at the action.

A steady stream of Higgins boats shuttled between the transports and the shore of Tulagi, the small island which, because of its deep and well-protected natural harbor, had been the seat of the British Solomon Islands Protectorate. A few fires burned on the beach and plumes of smoke rose from inland—vestiges of the pre-landing bombardment—but there was no sign of any fighting.

A mile and a half to the east, however, where marines had landed on the the tiny island of Gavutu, the defenders were putting up fierce resistance—how fierce could only be imagined. Faulkner hoped that the untested Yanks would prove equal to the battle-seasoned enemy soldiers.

The marines on Tulagi also soon met fierce opposition and were forced to halt their advance and dig in before sunset. Meanwhile the fighting on Gavutu spread to even smaller Tanambogo, linked to it by a narrow causeway. Tulagi and its two tiny neighbors introduced the kind of combat that would characterize much of the war to come: a costly assault against heavily dug-in Japanese troops determined to fight to the last man. Most of the Japanese defenders on Tulagi—only about 350 men—were hidden in coral caves and tunnels that proved almost impervious to naval gunnery or aerial bombardment.

(Above) The U.S. Navy Wildcat fighter lacked the grace and agility of the Zero, but its sturdy frame could take far more punishment.

it was estimated the planes would arrive in slightly over two hours. On board *Canberra*, the ship's loudspeaker system called all hands to dinner at 1100 and announced that an air attack was expected at noon—their first real action of the war.

With Mason's radio warning, a network of men known as the coastwatchers now came into its own. The coastwatchers were mostly British or Australian citizens who had lived in the islands for years. Before the Japanese invaded the eastern Solomons in early May, most of the European residents had left. But the coastwatchers took to the hills to act as a kind of early warning system of enemy military actions. Shifting location as deemed necessary—the teleradios were so large and heavy that they required twelve to sixteen men to carry the components through the bush—and relying on a network of loyal Melanesian natives for local intelligence, the coastwatchers proved of incalculable value in this early phase of the Guadalcanal campaign. Thanks to their efforts, few Japanese air attacks would take the Allies by surprise.

Sakai and the rest of the airplane attacking force were about fifty miles from Guadalcanal when he saw flashes of yellow flame piercing the tropical blue sky. Apparently the advance wave of attackers was already receiving a warm welcome. As he drew closer he looked down on the vast enemy fleet—more warships and transports than he had ever before seen together—and all of them showing white wakes, which meant they were already on the move, the standard tactic to make themselves more difficult targets. As the bombers entered a slow turn to prepare for their attack run, Sakai caught his first glimpse of the enemy fighter plane he would soon come to know well—the Grumman F4F, or Wildcat. Eight of them, in fact, painted blue-gray above and light gray below and looking chubby and awkward, fell on the bombers. As Sakai and the other fighter pilots roared to their defense, more Wildcats joined the fray, and soon several Bettys were in flames. Rattled, the bomber pilots released their payloads while still four miles up, targeting the ships

SABURO SAKAI AND THE REST OF THE JAPANESE AIRplane striking force couldn't know it, but the time of their arrival over Guadalcanal was already known. At midmorning, as the pack of Bettys passed over Malabita Hill a few miles inland from the southeastern tip of Bougainville, a short, middle-aged Australian polished his spectacles, then counted the planes flying overhead. A few minutes later, at 1037, the following message crackled from his bulky teleradio: "Twenty-four bombers headed yours." The man, whose name was Paul Mason and who had been born in Sydney, Australia, but had lived in the Solomons most of his life, would soon become known for such laconic but timely warnings. Within twenty-five minutes every ship in the fleet lying off Guadalcanal and Tulagi knew that the first Japanese counterattack was on its way. Based on the

COASTWATCHERS

A varied collection of planters and colonial officials kept tabs on the Japanese and aided the American invasion.

When the Japanese swept into the eastern Solomons in early May 1942, the coastwatchers on Guadalcanal suddenly found themselves operating behind enemy lines.

This was not the way it was supposed to be. The Australian Coastwatching Service had been set up by the Royal Australian Navy following World War I as a kind of early warning system against a future invasion of Australia. By the outbreak of war in 1939 the string of coastwatcher stations formed a 2,500-mile

long arc that stretched from the western end of Papua to the port of Vila on the island of Efate in the New Hebrides. With the Japanese advance, however, the coastwatchers on Guadalcanal became, in effect, spies who could expect no mercy if captured.

At Aola, District Officer Martin Clemens watched Tulagi and the eastern part of the island. A young and urbane Cambridge graduate, Clemens fended off boredom by re-reading his complete set of Shakespeare. To keep up morale, he organized a cricket match for his loyal native employees. High up on Gold Ridge, Lieutenant Donald Macfarlan, an Australian navy intelligence officer who was new to the area, surveyed the island's center from a comfortable five-bedroom house formerly occupied by the mine manager. He was soon joined by a local planter named Kenneth Hay, a man of great girth and epicurean habits. (Hay brought with him his kerosene-powered Electrolux refrigerator and even insisted that his butter be served

(Left) Martin Clemens (standing, fifth from left) and some of his scouts. (Below) In late May while waiting for the Japanese to land on Guadalcanal, Clemens passed the time by re-reading his three-volume complete plays of Shakespeare. (Right) Coastwatchers, for once wearing uniforms, stand

outside their headquarters on Guadalcanal. Among them is Snowy Rhoades (fourth from right). Coastwatchers lugged cumbersome radios like this one (right) with them to communicate with the outside world.

manager of a coconut plantation kept watch. He was F. A. "Snowy" Rhoades, a dour and laconic personality who had lived on the island for years.

In late June, when the Japanese landed in force on Guadalcanal and began constructing the airstrip, the situation of these four very different men became increasingly precarious as they moved to ever more remote and primitive hideouts hoping to escape detection. By late July, the situation appeared desperate. Clemens's carriers had deserted him, making it impossible to move his teleradio — it had broken down anyway — and his last pair of shoes had finally worn out. Macfarlan, who had retreated to a remote valley where the sun seldom shone, was running out of food. And Rhoades was living in a cave where he slept with "a pistol under his pillow." It was clear the Japanese were on their trail and that it was only a matter of time before they were captured. For the coastwatchers on Guadalcanal, the Allied invasion on

The coastwatchers also saved downed aviators and stranded sailors, the most famous of whom was John F. Kennedy (below), rescued by coastwatcher Arthur Reginald Evans after his ship, PT-109, was sunk in August 1943.

just southeast of Savo Island. Not one scored a hit.

While the Japanese bombers turned for home, the Zeros and Wildcats engaged in a series of acrobatic dogfights in which the Zero proved its superior maneuverability and the Wildcat its stubborn sturdiness. Sakai shortly spotted one Wildcat that appeared to be pursuing three Zeros (in fact the Wildcat pilot, whose plane was damaged, was simply trying to stay airborne until he could bail out over friendly territory). He dove to the attack, firing a desperate burst. The Wildcat rolled away, turned tightly and then climbed under Sakai. (This was Sakai's own favorite tactic—an attack from below—and he admired the American's flying skill.) There ensued a deadly aerial duet of lightning turns, sudden shifts in throttle and bone-crushing spirals until Sakai's adversary seemed to give up the fight, flying level and making no attempt to evade further attack. The Japanese ace pumped round after round into the cockpit, yet amazingly the enemy pilot kept flying.

As Sakai closed in for the final kill, there occurred one of those moments when, in the heat of battle, the enemy suddenly becomes human. The Wildcat's cockpit canopy had been blasted back and, as the two planes flew side by side, Sakai opened his cockpit window and stared at a big older man with a round face wearing a light khaki uniform. There was a bloodstain on his right shoulder and another on his chest. Sakai himself later recalled what happened next: "But this was no way to kill a man! Not with him flying helplessly, his plane a wreck. I raised my left hand and shook my fist at him, shouting, uselessly, I knew, for him to fight instead of just flying along like a clay pigeon. The American looked startled; he raised his right hand and weakly waved."

But then, as the American somehow pulled his plane into an upward loop, Sakai's fighting instincts returned. One carefully aimed burst from his cannon and the Grumman's engine exploded into smoke and flame. Then the plane rolled and the pilot bailed out. When the American's parachute snapped open, Sakai could see that the man's body hung lifelessly.

Sakai's adversary in this extraordinary episode was Lieutenant James J. "Pug" Southerland from Admiral Fletcher's flagship, Saratoga. Miraculously, he lived to tell the tale and fight again. Many of his comrades were not so lucky. Half of the eighteen Wildcats that engaged the enemy were lost. But the Japanese suffered more

A *Guadalcanal-bound Douglas Dauntless takes off from the flight deck of the U.S.S.* Enterprise. *An effective dive bomber, the Dauntless could also put up a defense against enemy fighters, thanks to its rear-mounted machine guns.*

heavily, losing nine Vals, as well as five Bettys and two Zeros. In return they scored only one hit, on destroyer *Mugford*, whose afterdeck house and two stern 5-inch guns were destroyed.

Meanwhile Sakai's own luck had run out. Mistaking a flight of Dauntless dive bombers for more Wildcats, he and another Zero attacked from the rear and below. Too late, he realized his mistake. The Dauntless with its rear machine gunner was much tougher game. Suddenly he was enveloped by enemy fire. The hit, when it came, felt as though someone had thrust a knife into each ear. The world suddenly turned red. Then he went blind.

SURGEON LIEUTENANT KENNETH MORRIS (NO relation to Tom Morris on *Quincy*) could barely breathe. He and the two sick-berth attendants stationed at the forward first-aid position on *Canberra's* forecastle mess deck had spent the entire air attack sweating in their heavy antiflash gear—overalls, gloves, helmets, goggles—while the air belowdecks in the closed-down ship became progressively more oppressive. At times like this one's imagination was as much the enemy as the Japanese. It tended to run wild.

The whole thing began with the firing of *Canberra's* 8-inch guns. They made such a racket that Morris thought for sure the ship had been hit by torpedoes, even though his rational mind knew the enemy planes must still be too far away to release their weapons. Then the rapidly firing 4-inch guns chimed in, followed by the two-pounder pom-poms—the planes were getting closer, but how close he could only guess. The chatter of the Oerlikon 20 mm automatic anti-aircraft guns indicated the enemy had to be dropping bombs and torpedoes—and surely one was bound to find the mark. Finally, as *Canberra's* machine guns started to rattle, he knew the planes were bearing in on the ship. Perhaps one was about to crash into the superstructure. If a hit was going to come, it would be any second . . . .

Suddenly the racket stopped. The all clear sounded. The danger had passed. As he removed his gear and wiped away the sweat, Morris couldn't help checking to make sure it really was just perspiration and not blood. If only one could see what was going on, it wouldn't be so bad.

On board the Allied ships, the failure of the first Japanese air attack added to the general feeling of

(cont'd on page 39)

The heavy cruiser H.M.A.S. Canberra *was built in Great Britain before the war and prior to Guadalcanal had chased German raiders in the Indian Ocean.*

AWAY ALL BOATS

The first major American amphibious landing since the Spanish-American War was an improvised and under-rehearsed affair.

The Allied commanders in charge of the invasion didn't know what to expect. Estimates as to the size of the Japanese forces on Tulagi and Guadalcanal varied widely (from as little as 3,100 to over 8,000). Reconnaissance was sketchy: there wasn't even a complete topographic map and a detailed air photo mosaic of Guadalcanal had gotten lost in the mail from Australia. Intelligence analysts guessed that the

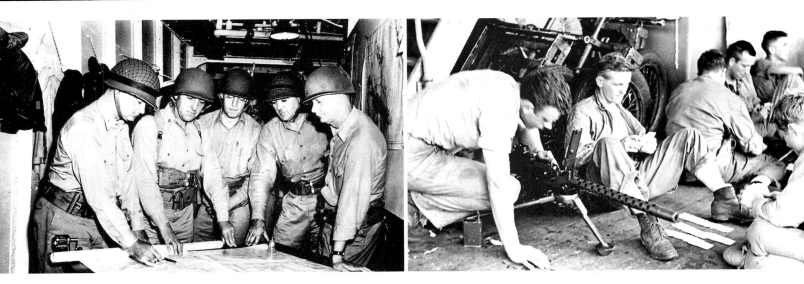

enemy forces were concentrated around the still-incomplete airfield. In fact they were almost all on Tulagi.

Most of the marines (many of whom had enlisted in the burst of patriotic fervor following Pearl Harbor) were barely out of boot camp. Their only dress rehearsal, at Koro in the Fiji Islands, had been a disaster thanks to unplanned-for coral reefs and motor failures in the landing craft. (Admiral Turner cancelled the exercise after only a third had disembarked.) The rifle regiments carried the same weapon an earlier generation had used in World War I, the M-1903 Springfield bolt action rifle. If the enemy had been well entrenched and had put up a serious fight on the beach, the casualties would surely have been horrendous.

(Far left) General Vandegrift and his staff meet on board ship to complete planning for the invasion while (near left) his marines clean their weapons and wait. (Right) The designated landing zone was called Beach Red. From it they were to move west and inland to secure the airstrip. Most of the transports were converted liners, although fast destroyer transports (left) were

also used. (Top) Amphibious tractors hauled in supplies, but most troops came ashore in landing craft (above). (Right) Marines make their way inland.

Landing craft snake in toward shore on August 7, 1942. (Inset) A. Archer Vandegrift, commander of the First Marine Division. By late afternoon, Vandegrift followed his division ashore and set up his headquarters on Guadalcanal.

confidence. None of the transports had been hit, and only those on board the damaged destroyer had any foretaste of the nasty meal that was soon to come. Through the remainder of the afternoon, the landings on Guadalcanal continued unopposed. At 4 P.M. General Vandegrift moved his headquarters ashore, while expressing extreme frustration at the tortoiselike progress of the American landing force. By nightfall the prong of the marine advance moving along the coast would make it only as far as Alligator Creek (also known as the Ilu River), still a thousand yards from the airfield. A second prong became mired deep in the jungle.

The word from General William Rupertus, commander of the Tulagi landing force, was that fierce fighting continued on Tulagi and Gavutu-Tanambogo. Casualties were heavy. Vandegrift must have wondered how long the marines' honeymoon on Guadalcanal would last.

SABURO SAKAI REGAINED CONSCIOUSNESS JUST AS HIS plane was about to crash into the water and, although still blind from blood, he managed to right the Zero by sheer instinct. But his whole left side seemed to be paralyzed. Tears washed away enough blood for him to see his instruments dimly, but his situation seemed hopeless. It was more than five hundred miles to Rabaul. His cockpit cover was gone, the plane was surely seriously damaged, and he was in need of immediate medical attention. Somehow he managed to work his silk flier's scarf up and under his helmet to help stanch the flow of blood and to position a seat cushion as a windbreak.

Slouched as low as possible to avoid the onrushing wind, and unable to see where he was going, Sakai now found himself fighting the desire to sleep. Time and again he dozed off, starting awake to find himself flying upside down or almost crashing into the waves. He tried hitting himself on his wounded cheek, hoping the pain would help him maintain consciousness, but this only caused his face to bloat out, as if a rubber ball were growing inside his mouth. "If I must die," he began to say to himself, "at least I will go out as a Samurai." More than once he turned back toward Guadalcanal to look for an enemy ship to crash into, then changed his mind and reversed course for Rabaul. But each backtrack wasted precious fuel, making his safe return more and more unlikely. At one point he came out of his stupor to

realize that for some time he had been flying north into the empty Pacific. Finally, with the increasing pain from his head wound now keeping him awake, he regained his bearings and headed once and for all for Rabaul, flying at minimum speed to conserve fuel.

After what seemed like many hours, Sakai spotted the familiar volcanic peaks of New Britain, but the direct route over its mountainous interior seemed too perilous, so he decided to skirt the coast, following St. George's Channel between Rabaul and New Ireland. As he entered the channel he glanced below him to see the white wakes of two cruisers heading rapidly southeast. He hoped they were headed for Guadalcanal.

A few minutes later, the airfield at Rabaul was at last in his sights, but he and his plane were both near their limits. He circled, debating whether to ditch in the water just off the beach. The thought of a bone-jolting crash into the water was too much to bear, so he determined to attempt a landing. His first try almost ended in disaster when he missed the runway and nearly crashed into the parked fighters. Pulling up, he circled four times and then went in for another try. His fuel gauge read empty, but he was taking no chances of an engine fire on crash landing. When he cleared the palms at the edge of the runway he switched off the ignition with a kick of his right boot (his left leg was still useless). A few seconds later the plane hit the ground with a jolting thud and rolled to a halt in front of the command post. As his mind let go and he fell into blackness he heard shouts of "Sakai! Sakai!"

"I cursed to myself," he later recalled. "Why didn't they keep quiet? I wanted to sleep."

SLEEP WAS A SCARCE COMMODITY THAT FIRST NIGHT on Guadalcanal, as war correspondent Richard Tregaskis discovered. "Bedding down for the night under the tall palms and a panoply of soft stars would have been a beautiful experience," he wrote in his diary, "except for bugs, mosquitoes and thirst—which unfortunately were all too present. With the coming of the dark, the mackaws [sic] began to squeal in the treetops, and rifle shots became more numerous. The sentries were jittery on this their first night on the island. I awoke from time to time to hear the call of 'Halt!' followed almost immediately by volleys of gunfire. Once, near midnight, I woke to hear a sub-machine gun cracking very near the grove. Then a rifle barked. Then another. And soon, five or six guns were firing simultaneously, and the bright white tracer bullets were zipping in several directions over the grove where we slept. Some of the slugs whined through the trees close by. And then the firing fell off, and died, and we went back to sleep again."

Others found the Guadalcanal night more ominous. Private Robert Leckie allowed his imagination to get the better of him: "I could hear the darkness gathering against me and the silences that lay between the moving things. I could hear the enemy everywhere about me, whispering to each other and calling my name. I lay open mouthed and half-mad beneath that giant tree. I had not looked into its foliage before darkness and now I fancied it infested with Japanese . . . ."

Over on Tulagi, where the enemy was not imaginary, the Japanese garrison staged several fierce counterattacks, some of them infiltrating behind the marine lines. When morning came the bodies of dead Japanese lay yards from the American defensive lines. The pockets of infiltrators were wiped out soon after dawn.

VICE ADMIRAL MIKAWA, though not an easy man to ruffle, had good reason to be uneasy as he paced the bridge of his flagship, the heavy cruiser *Chokai*. Daylight on August 8 would expose his naval striking force—now lurking east of the big island of Bougainville—to probing enemy eyes. And to add to his discomfort, the route to Guadalcanal would take his eight ships through poorly charted waters holding who knew what unmarked shoals. Nonetheless, if the Allied landings were to be defeated, his ships were the only force that could do it. His daring plan

Vice Admiral Gunichi Mikawa, commander of the Japanese Eighth Fleet, believed he could stop the American invasion —if he could arrive off Guadalcanal undetected.

was to race southeastward and attack the Americans near midnight, disabling their warships and destroying the transports, then vanishing well before dawn. The Japanese navy specialized in night fighting, so he felt confident on that score, but until nightfall he was vulnerable to enemy aircraft from the American carriers whose planes had parried the first Japanese air attack on the landing force, but had so far eluded reconnaissance as they maneuvered somewhere south of Guadalcanal.

On Mikawa's orders, at 0600, just as the first light streaked the eastern sky, five seaplanes leapt from their catapults on board his cruisers and headed off to reconnoiter the situation at Guadalcanal and Tulagi. Two and a half hours later they reported. Despite the optimistic claims of the bomber pilots, the air attack of the previous day had not discernibly affected the invasion fleet. The Allies remained off Guadalcanal in force, superior in numbers and in firepower. And given that he would have to show his hand and begin steaming at high speed toward his objective, it seemed impossible that he could do so undetected.

At 1025, with his force now just northeast of Kieta on Bougainville, Mikawa's fears were realized. A Hudson bomber appeared and began shadowing the Japanese ships. The admiral promptly ordered a left turn to throw the pilot off the scent, steaming northwest as if back for Rabaul until the plane departed. A few minutes later a second Hudson appeared, flying low over the water, but was driven off by Japanese 8-inch guns.

The Australian crew of the first Hudson to sight Mikawa's task force had initially mistaken it as friendly, until flashes of gunfire answered their signal lamp.

The pilot, Sergeant William Stutt, knew his orders under such circumstances and followed them to the letter. He instructed his radio operator, Sergeant Eric Geddes, to break radio silence and report the sighting. Their home base at Milne Bay on the southeastern tip of New Guinea was too far away to get the message. And how soon it reached Admiral Turner remains a moot point. But by early evening the American commander of the ships off Guadalcanal knew of the two Hudson sightings. The first reported two destroyers, three cruisers, and two "gunboats or seaplane tenders." The second said the Japanese force consisted of "two heavy cruisers, two light cruisers and an unidentified vessel." Neither of these messages suggested a naval force strong enough to take on the Allied fleet protecting the landings.

Radio operators on *Chokai* had monitored the first Hudson's sighting report, but Admiral Mikawa did not change his plans, even though he had to assume that his arrival at Guadalcanal that night would be expected. He turned again to the southeast, hoping against hope that he would be able to evade the inevitable attack from carrier-based planes. By early afternoon his force had emerged from the tricky confines of Bougainville Strait into the open waters of the long wide channel the Americans would nickname the Slot, where he would have a better chance in an air attack. It was now clear sailing and speed was increased to 24 knots. Mikawa's bravado was rewarded. He steamed down the Slot all afternoon without being detected.

Admiral Turner and his superior Admiral Fletcher had both noted serious weaknesses in the Allied aerial reconnaisance plan that day. To summarize a very complex situation, much of the Slot would be left uncovered all afternoon. An enemy force could thus enter this natural approach route to Guadalcanal in time to reach the island at night without detection (which is exactly what happened). To rectify this situation, both admirals requested additional flights over the area—flights that either weren't flown or didn't fly far enough. Of this fatal lapse, however, both Turner and Fletcher were unaware.

Rear Admiral R. Kelly Turner, the American commander, feared a naval counterattack. Despite his request for extra air patrols, the likely route of a Japanese approach was inadequately covered.

ENSIGN HARRIS HAMMERSMITH SAT IN THE COCKPIT OF his SOC scout biplane preparing for launch from *Quincy's* starboard catapult. In the cockpit immediately behind him, his radioman/gunner was also securely strapped in. Hammersmith moved the throttle forward to full power and signaled to the catapult operator that he was ready. Then he pushed the throttle as far as it would go—maximum power—as the small plane strained against its restraints. The catapult operator waited a few moments for the ship to begin a roll to port (the rising starboard side would give the plane some extra lift) then snapped the lanyard that released the ignition charge. With a sound like a 5-inch gun firing and a feeling he would later describe as being "like a great big boot in the butt," the plane shot forward and he was airborne. At last.

The release was doubly exhilarating because of the pent-up frustration that had preceded it. All day on August 7, Hammersmith had played the role of spectator while the more senior *Quincy* pilots flew spotting runs for the shipboard guns and newly landed shore artillery. That first night at Guadalcanal he had dreamed only of flying his biplane.

Now he headed toward the eastern entrance to the sound, a series of channels between Guadalcanal and Florida Island, where he was to patrol for enemy submarines. To his right he could see that Beach Red was covered with men and mounds of food and equipment. An enemy air attack now, he reflected, could be devastating.

For the next four hours Hammersmith methodically flew his search pattern above the turquoise water patterned with barely submerged coral reefs. Over on Tulagi

(Below left) Japanese Betty bombers, some just a few feet above the water, race in for the attack on the transports. (Below right) Smoke rises from a burning transport.

and its two tiny neighbors there were still signs of fighting, but the shallow waters that made a sub easy to spot betrayed no trace of the enemy. Finally, with about forty-five minutes' worth of fuel remaining, he turned to head back home. That was when he realized the Japanese airplanes were back.

As Hammersmith drew closer, he could see that the main action was concentrated on the warships screening the transports, although one transport (this turned out to be *George F. Elliot*) was on fire. Then one of the destroyers took a torpedo hit, a great geyser of flame rising at her bow (this was *Jarvis*). The sky was filled with flak and many enemy planes were falling to anti-aircraft fire and to the defending Wildcats. It looked as if the Allied side was winning.

Hammersmith brought his float plane down until it was skimming a few yards above the water and piloted slow S-curves to evade enemy fire. (Unarmored and with a maximum speed of 165 miles per hour he knew he was no match for speedy Zeros.) But his fuel gauge was close to empty and this was not the time to head back to *Quincy*, busy fending off the air attack. He concluded that his best option would be to land near Beach Red.

(Below) A faint column of smoke, probably from the burning transport George F. Elliot, can be seen to the left of the U.S.S. Chicago in the background. Our 1992 expedition found craters in the sea bottom caused by the Bettys' bombs.

*(Top left and right) Although manned by well-trained, seasoned crews, Betty bombers had one serious drawback —
their fuel tanks had no protection against anti-aircraft fire. As a result, the planes easily caught fire and crashed.
(Above) A Betty bomber, minus tail, photographed from the destroyer* Ellet.

From there he could probably be picked up later. As the distant cruisers spat anti-aircraft fire and more enemy planes burst into flames, he settled his floats into the water and taxied up to the beach.

For Able Seaman Henry Hall on *Canberra* the war was about to become rather immediate. From his battle station in forward control, a windowed space just above and behind the open compass platform of the bridge and just below the 8-inch gun director, he had a good view of the action and not much to do. During a surface engagement he operated the inclinometer for the forward 8-inch guns. This was a device for determining a target's angle of approach and whether it was altering course, but it was useless during an air attack and now he was little more than a spectator. All the ship's ordnance was firing and she shuddered with each blast. The big guns were loaded with barrage fuses set to explode after a fixed interval. Hall watched as a Betty headed directly at him, flying low over the water and ready to release its torpedo. Then an 8-inch shell exploded nearby and the plane literally disintegrated before his eyes, pieces of fuselage fluttering aimlessly down to the water. The sight made him think of a popular song called "Autumn Leaves," a melancholy evocation of the end of summer. Then he realized there had been human beings inside that airplane. "Well, it's either them or us," he thought grimly.

From his bleacher seat on Beach Red, Harris Hammersmith waited for the air attack to end. He didn't have enough gas to take off, let alone get back to *Quincy*, so it looked as if he'd have to spend the night ashore. Then he had a bright idea, which he explained to a skeptical marine captain. It took all his powers of

From his battle station on the Canberra, *Henry Hall had a clear view of the Japanese air attacks on August 8.*

persuasion, but in the end the captain let him have ten gallons of tank fuel—enough to fly him safely back to his ship. By the time he took off, the air attack was over and the Higgins boats were once again beetling between the transports and the Guadalcanal beach, as the unloading continued.

This second Japanese air attack on the invasion force had proved as ineffectual and costly as the previous day's. Although this time a transport, *George F. Elliot*, had been damaged, the landing of supplies continued until dark, then ceased on Admiral Turner's orders due to the continuing bottleneck on the beach. On Guadalcanal, the marines had finally reached the airfield, which revealed just how completely the enemy had been surprised by the Allied invasion. Uneaten breakfasts sat on tables inside mess tents, and vast arrays of stores—food, weapons and construction equipment—had been abandoned. (Contrary to General Vandegrift's expectations, there had been only a small detachment of Japanese combat troops on Guadalcanal; the rest were construction workers, of whom most were Koreans impressed into Japanese service.)

Fighting would continue on and near Tulagi for several days, but by sunset on August 8, organized resistance had ceased. All the primary objectives were achieved. It had almost been too easy.

Admiral Turner, however, was far from pleased. In fact he was about ready to explode. He had just learned that Admiral Fletcher was pulling out his three aircraft carriers, leaving Turner's ships dangerously exposed. From the beginning Fletcher had expressed grave misgivings about the whole operation. (He had already lost aircraft carriers at Midway and in the Battle of the Coral Sea and wasn't about to lose another.) It had taken all Turner's and Vandegrift's persuasive powers to convince their boss to agree to remain off Guadalcanal for three days. Now the expeditionary force commander had concluded the Japanese torpedo planes posed an unacceptable threat to his flattops and decided to take them out of danger a full day early. Before morning, they would be well out of range.

As dusk fell, Turner summoned General Vandegrift and Admiral Victor Crutchley (who was in tactical command of the warships supporting the landings) to a meeting aboard his flagship, the transport U.S.S. *McCawley*. He would have bad news for the marine commander. Without the protection of carrier-based planes, the only prudent course was a withdrawal of all the ships now at Guadalcanal.

Crutchley received Turner's summons aboard his flagship, heavy cruiser *Australia*, which led a patrol group guarding the southwestern entrance to the sound. The British admiral, who had only recently been seconded from

(Above) Victor Crutchley, whom the Australians nicknamed "Old Goat Whiskers," met with Turner and Vandegrift (below) to discuss the impending withdrawal of the American carriers.

the Royal Navy to the Royal Australian Navy, was in charge of the warships protecting the transports against a nocturnal surface attack. To this end he had divided his forces into three groups, one each to cover the three possible routes the enemy might take.

The sound's southwestern entrance was one of the two most likely approaches. Along with *Australia*, the group guarding this passage consisted of the heavy cruisers *Chicago* and *Canberra* sailing in formation with destroyers *Bagley* and *Patterson*. These ships were steaming back and forth in the channel south of Savo on a roughly twelve-mile-long northwest/southeast line, running parallel to the Guadalcanal coastline.

Guarding the other likely route of attack, the slightly wider northwestern entrance between Savo and Florida islands, was the responsibility of Captain Frederick Riefkohl, commander of the heavy cruiser *Vincennes*. *Vincennes*, together with heavy cruisers *Quincy* and *Astoria* and destroyers *Helm* and *Wilson*, sailed in a box-like patrol pattern at a speed of 10 knots, turning the corner every thirty minutes.

Meanwhile Rear Admiral Norman Scott's force, the light cruisers *San Juan* and *Hobart* and the destroyers *Monssen* and *Buchanan*, watched the eastern approaches, which because of their narrowness presented an improbable route for a major attack but were quite passable for submarines, destroyers or motor torpedo boats. Finally, working as lone sentinels beyond the two western approaches were destroyers *Blue*, outside the southwestern entrance, and *Ralph Talbot*, outside the northwestern. Both were equipped with an early form of radar—something the Japanese still lacked—but its effectiveness was poorly understood and greatly diminished by the proximity of land. Each of these two pickets traversed a 6 1/2-mile line, but their timing wasn't coordinated, creating

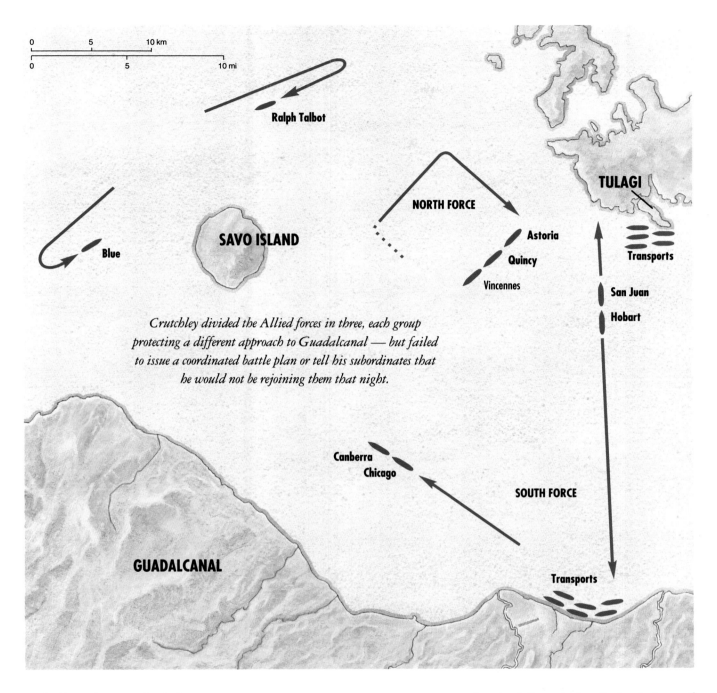

Scale bar:
0 — 5 — 10 km
0 — 5 — 10 mi

Ralph Talbot

SAVO ISLAND

Blue

NORTH FORCE

Astoria

Quincy

Vincennes

TULAGI

Transports

San Juan

Hobart

Crutchley divided the Allied forces in three, each group protecting a different approach to Guadalcanal — but failed to issue a coordinated battle plan or tell his subordinates that he would not be rejoining them that night.

Canberra

Chicago

SOUTH FORCE

GUADALCANAL

Transports

---

periodic major gaps in their coverage.

Crutchley now informed the number two man in his patrol group, *Chicago*'s Captain Howard Bode, that he was leaving to meet with Turner, then pulled *Australia* out of formation and headed for the transports anchored off Beach Red. But he failed to inform his other subordinate commanders of his departure and he seems to have left Captain Bode with the impression his absence would be brief. This would explain Bode's decision to retain *Chicago*'s station behind *Canberra* rather than taking the lead, the normal position for a command ship, whose

movements can then be followed visually in the heat of battle. Worse, Crutchley left the three guard groups without knowledge of each other's patrol patterns and with no clear battle plan in the event a Japanese attack materialized.

JUST BEFORE SUNSET, THE SHIPS IN ADMIRAL Mikawa's striking force jettisoned everything flammable from their exposed decks and formed into night battle order. His flagship, *Chokai*, took the lead. The rest of the fleet followed in single file 3/4 of a mile

apart. Then, as the sun sank behind them, Mikawa signaled each ship with a conscious echo of Lord Nelson's famous message at Trafalgar: "In the finest tradition of the Imperial Navy we shall engage the enemy in night battle. Every man is expected to do his best."

One of those who listened to this exhortation was Kurato Yoshiie, a twenty-four-year-old searchlight operator aboard *Chokai*. Yoshiie had joined the navy at age seventeen and had been on the heavy cruiser during the successful invasion of the Malay Peninsula and the triumphal fall of Singapore. Like most of his fellows, he had been swept up in the euphoria of Japan's early victories and believed his country's soldiers and sailors to be invincible. But recently doubts had begun to enter his mind. He and his mates had heard rumors of the terrible losses

at the Battle of Midway. Now the Americans had actually attacked an island held by Japanese forces. And the friendly airplanes they had seen a few hours earlier, returning from the day's sortie against the enemy landing forces, were so depleted in number that they didn't even bother trying to fly in formation. The dinner of cold beans and rice sat heavily in his stomach. He hadn't been hungry, but he had eaten every morsel so as not to displease his watching division commander. Now he wondered if the meal would prove to be his last.

THE THREE MEN WHO SAT IN THE WARM LIGHT OF THE wardroom of U.S.S. *McCawley*, anchored with the other transports off Lunga Point, were glum. Behind Admiral Turner's wire-rimmed glasses his eyes

(Above) Kurato Yoshiie (standing with an unidentified friend) had served on Admiral Mikawa's flagship, the heavy cruiser Chokai (left and below), during the successful invasion of Malaya and the fall of Singapore.

were tired, his customary schoolmasterish manner subdued as he explained the implications of Admiral Fletcher's withdrawal with his aircraft carriers. Admiral Crutchley stroked his flame-red beard and agreed with Turner's assessment. It would be unwise to expose the landing force to Japanese air attack without Fletcher's air support. The best course would be to pull out the next morning. General Vandegrift, whose gentle Virginia drawl was in stark contrast to Crutchley's clipped English accent, noted that both admirals looked completely exhausted. (Crutchley had not yet even found time to meet with all the American officers under his command.) Vandegrift expressed alarm at the prospect of being left to fend for himself with only a portion of his supplies unloaded, but he could not dispute the

logic of the admirals' position. Before a final decision was made, however, he requested permission to take a firsthand look at the situation on Tulagi, where bloody fighting continued. Accordingly, just before midnight, Vandegrift boarded the destroyer minesweeper *Southard* and headed across the silent sound.

The three men also discussed the morning Hudson sighting of Mikawa's naval force, but both Turner and Crutchley had by now concluded that these enemy ships represented no immediate threat, assuming, erroneously, that the additional air searches requested for that day had been carried out. Based on the first report of "seaplane tenders," Turner had concluded the enemy was bent on establishing a seaplane base. He assumed it would be at Rekata Bay on the northwest coast of Santa Isabel, one hundred miles to the northwest, from which the Japanese would probably launch air attacks the next morning—August 9. This was a fatal mistake, a failure to assume the worst possibility until proven otherwise.

Just how complacent Turner and Crutchley were is indicated by the British admiral's subsequent actions. When Crutchley rejoined *Australia*, snugly anchored inside the destroyer screen guarding the Guadalcanal transports, he went to bed without even bothering to inform Captain Bode or his other subordinate commanders that he would not be returning to his patrol position until morning. Captain Riefkohl in *Vincennes* was now the senior officer of the two western patrol groups, theoretically in overall tactical command if the Japanese attacked, but he didn't know it.

JUST AFTER 11 P.M. ADMIRAL MIKAWA AGAIN launched his floatplanes. He worried that his pilots had no experience of night catapulting, but there were no mishaps. Just before midnight he ordered white streamers hoisted to the signal yards to mark his ships to each other. Then he increased speed from 24 to 26 knots. The first floatplane reports indicated enemy cruisers sailing south of Savo Island. At midnight he issued the order to man battle stations and turned the speed up another notch to 28 knots. The dark, silent shapes knifed through the tropical night, almost invisible except for the white foaming at the bows and the white churning wakes. Clouds and frequent rainsqualls obscured the stars. The moon had not yet risen and the darkness was complete. The Japanese fleet was now flying to its destiny—to death or to glory for the emperor.

CHAPTER THREE

THE WORST DEFEAT

August 8, 1942

BOARD H.M.A.S. *CANBERRA*, THE EIGHT-TO-midnight watch on August 8 was a quiet one. The Australian crewmen were exhausted from the past two and a half days, during which most of them had lived at or near their action stations. Now with the ship at one rung below maximum readiness, the majority were relaxing as best they could. Surgeon Lieutenant Kenneth Morris, for example, lay down on a mess table and was soon fast asleep (his two orderlies followed suit). Stoker Second Class George Faulkner, sweating out his final hour of duty in the after engine room, counted the minutes until he could head for a shower and then his hammock. And in the handling room for Y turret, the aftermost of the four 8-inch turrets, Able Seaman Stephen St. George and several others had removed their heavy antiflash gear and were playing cards.

Just before midnight Sub-Lieutenant Mackenzie Gregory made his way to *Canberra*'s bridge to assume his duties as an officer of the midnight-to-four watch. He noted that Savo Island was shrouded in a rainsquall and that mist hung in the air around the ship, somewhat reducing visibility. But he could clearly make out the two escorting destroyers, *Patterson* and *Bagley*, to port and starboard, their wakes gleaming with phosphorescence. Although he couldn't see *Chicago*, Gregory knew the heavy cruiser was about 600 yards astern, matching *Canberra* step for step. Thunder rumbled in the distance.

Several miles to the north, the mood on U.S.S. *Quincy* was equally subdued. Captain Samuel Moore, like the commanders on all the Allied ships, had already turned in, although his emergency cabin was only a few steps

American cruisers under fire in what one historian called the worst "blue-water defeat" in American naval history.

away from the bridge. As far as he knew, the night promised routine patrolling, nothing more.

About 1145, Quartermaster Second Class Thomas Morris went to rouse Lieutenant Commander Edmund Billings, who was due to assume command of the watch at midnight. Billings was one of the older officers on board—he had been a chief petty officer during World War I—and sometimes he overslept. When roused, Billings' first words were, "Son, is there any action on the bridge?" "No, everything is quiet, sir," Morris told him. A few minutes later, when Morris rechecked to make sure the lieutenant commander was fully awake, Billings, who was already puffing on his ever-present pipe, again asked if there was any activity on the bridge. Apparently he was less willing than the captain to assume that the Japanese would not attack that night. "Nothing to report, sir," Morris replied.

Midnight passed and the Japanese striking force charged onward, unseen and unsuspected. At 1240 a lookout on *Chokai* spotted the unmistakable shape of Savo Island just off the port bow. All eyes on the bridge searched the night for some sign of the enemy. Suddenly a lookout called out, "Ship approaching, 30 degrees starboard." It was a destroyer a little over six miles ahead, on a course across *Chokai's* bow. (This was in fact *Blue*, one of the two destroyer pickets patrolling west of Savo.)

A less cool commander might have opened fire, but Admiral Mikawa paused an interminable moment, then quietly ordered, "Left rudder, slow to 22 knots." The slower speed would make his ships' wakes less visible. Best to assume he had not been seen until given evidence to the contrary. On *Chokai's* bridge, the watchers waited.

The Allied destroyer continued blithely on, giving no sign that it had detected the Japanese presence. Then, to the delight and amazement of the attackers, it reversed course and headed off in the opposite direction. But almost instantly relief gave way to renewed tension when another ship was sighted, this time off the port bow. It, however, was steaming away to the northeast and it too gave no sign of having sighted the Japanese. (This was not the other destroyer picket, *Ralph Talbot*, but an inter-island steamer that had inadvertently strayed into the battle zone.) Thus the striking force slipped undetected between the two destroyer sentries and headed for the southern entrance to the sound and the unwary cruisers *Canberra* and *Chicago*, with their two destroyers *Bagley* and *Patterson*.

(*Above*) *Within minutes of coming under fire the* Canberra *was hit dozens of times, including one shell that badly wounded her commanding officer, Captain Frank Getting (below).*

At about 0140, the dim shapes of enemy ships were sighted ahead and to starboard, at a range of five miles. Right on schedule a parachute flare from one of the Japanese float planes burst over the scene, turning night into day. On *Chokai*, Captain Mikio Hayakawa gave the order: "Torpedoes fire to starboard. Fire."

A S *CANBERRA* APPROACHED THE WESTERN END OF ITS patrol line, the darkened bridge was hushed. Most of the more senior officers were asleep. Sub-Lieutenant Gregory, who had assumed his watch duties on schedule at midnight, was preparing to call the navigator so he could fix the ship's position prior to the scheduled course change at 0200. Suddenly the calm was shattered by an explosion (presumably the first Japanese flare). Gregory had just checked the chart-table clock, which read 0143.

In *Canberra*'s fore control, above and aft of the bridge, Able Seaman Henry Hall was talking on the telephone to the person manning the phones on the 4-inch gun deck when a green-white flash lit the night. "Stupid bloody Yanks," he muttered. "What the hell are they up to?" It was beyond him why the Americans would be dropping flares. The next thing he knew, his telephone headset disintegrated and the man beside him, his face blasted by shrapnel, dropped down dead. Without thinking, Hall fell to his knees.

The men on *Canberra*'s bridge moved quickly once danger was detected, but their countermeasures were too little, too late. Captain Frank Getting arrived while the action alarms were sounding and was informed that torpedo tracks had been spotted off the port bow. The helmsman promptly turned the ship to starboard so the the main turrets could fire, but shells began to rain down before the guns were fully loaded. At least two shells landed near the bridge, killing the chief gunnery officer and badly wounding the captain (it was undoubtedly one of these shells that sent the shrapnel that almost killed Henry Hall). Other hits knocked out both boiler rooms and with them the ship's power. As she slid to a halt, her big guns were already useless. Several shells passed right through the hull, emerging to starboard

below the water line. Seawater began to pour into her innards.

Deep inside the stern of *Canberra*, between the forward propellers, Ordinary Seaman Albert Warne and the other men in the Y-turret shell room heard the hydraulic sound indicating that the 8-inch guns were being brought to bear. Suddenly Warne heard a series of muffled explosions culminating in a loud bang directly overhead, followed by a shower of sparks that somehow found their way past the tightly closed hatch. Sweat began pouring down his face and the antiflash gear became almost unbearably hot. If that shell had wiped out the crew above, who were supposed to open the hatch for them to escape in case of trouble, this small room had just become his tomb. Abruptly the ship's engine sounds died down. Then the lights began to fade as he listened to the propellers gradually stop turning.

Warne could barely discern the faces of the other men in the glimmer

(Top) Shell hits on the Canberra *knocked out all her power and nearly trapped Bert Warne (above) and his mates deep in the ship.*

of the single emergency lamp. No one spoke except to utter a brief expletive. Time passed. A minute, perhaps two, but it seemed much, much longer. Then the hatch above their heads clanged open, a head appeared and yelled "OUT!" The order did not need to be repeated.

On the forecastle mess deck, Surgeon Lieutenant Morris first realized the ship had been hit when wounded men came staggering in. He had barely begun to treat the first of these when the room was plunged into darkness. With only a flashlight attached to a headband for illumination, he did his best to patch and mend, losing all concept of time. When the order came to prepare to abandon ship, he and two sickberth attendants began the arduous task of carrying casualties up on deck.

Sub-Lieutenant Gregory reached his action station in the fore control area just before the ship lost power. Although shells seemed to be landing all around him, somehow he had made it this far without a scratch. Moments later his position took a near-miss, and the man standing beside him was badly wounded. With power gone and a huge fire now blazing amidships, he ordered those remaining to assist with the wounded and throw ammunition overboard before it caught fire and made things worse.

On the devastated compass platform of the bridge, Captain Getting refused all medical help until the other wounded were attended to, even though his right leg was shattered from the knee down. Chief Engineer McMahon arrived to report on the damage below. "Sir, I'm afraid things are bad," he said. "We've been hit in the engine room." Through the pain Getting managed to whisper a reply: "Do your best, Mac." But there was little that could be done.

For Ordinary Seaman Warne the real horror of the night began after he and his mates in the Y-turret shell room squeezed one by one through the hatch into the room above, only to discover that their likeliest means of escape—the wire-rope ladder up a narrow ventilation shaft—had been shot away. Now three perilous decks separated them from safety. They groped their way through the thickening smoke, occasionally lit by a wisp of flame from the burning deck covering. It gave off almost overpowering sulfur-like fumes that stung Warne's eyes and throat and hurt his lungs. With each passing minute it became more and more difficult to breathe. It was hard not to panic when squeezing through a narrow hatch in the smoke-filled dark. At one point Warne picked up a small emergency lantern he stumbled over, but its feeble light was useless and he tossed it away. As he neared the upper deck, the smoke began to clear and he passed many wounded men. When he finally reached the open air, he lay gulping the delicious oxygen as a gentle tropical shower fell. The rain seemed like God's blessing.

THE FIRST PHASE OF THE BATTLE HAD BEEN A PIGEON shoot for the Japanese. No torpedoes seem to have struck *Canberra* (this is still a topic of debate), but at least one blasted away a large chunk of *Chicago*'s bow. Although otherwise undamaged, *Chicago* had trouble bringing her guns to bear, and she began sailing westward, away from the battle. Thus, only minutes into the action both Allied cruisers were effectively out of the fight.

Mikawa now turned his cruisers north toward the group of ships patrolling the northwestern entrance to the sound. In the course of this maneuver his single battle line became split into two roughly parallel pincers—probably because the disabled *Canberra* stumbled into the path of *Furutaka*, the fourth ship in the Japanese line. At any rate, the eastern group consisted of *Chokai*, *Aoba*, *Kako* and *Kinugasa*; the western group of *Furutaka*, *Tenryu* and *Yubari*. (The lone Japanese destroyer, *Yunagi*, had been detached before the action and left to guard the rear.)

The only Allied ship from the southern patrol group to seriously engage the Japanese was the escorting destroyer *Patterson*, although damaged *Chicago* apparently scored one hit on *Tenryu* while retreating westward. (*Bagley* fired torpedoes, none of which hit, then also turned west.) *Patterson*'s two after 5-inch guns had been knocked out, but the crew battled the resulting fire to a standstill while Commander Frank Walker gave chase, scoring a hit on *Kinugasa* before receiving an order to proceed to a rendezvous with unengaged destroyers for a mass torpedo attack. (This order came from Admiral Crutchley, who had no idea what was actually going on, but was belatedly attempting to assert command from *Australia*, which was still anchored off Beach Red with the transports.) Walker earned an additional distinction in those frantic first moments. His was the only ship to send out a radio alert. At 0146, when he first sighted an enemy cruiser, he broadcast, "Warning! Warning! Strange ships entering harbor." Had the message been heeded, the northern patrol group might have been slightly better prepared for the firestorm that was about to hit them.

THE EXHAUSTED CAPTAINS OF THE THREE CRUISERS in the northern group—*Vincennes*, *Quincy* and *Astoria*—were still asleep in their sea cabins when the southern phase of the battle began. They were not roused despite the fact that their bridge watches had monitored several unidentified airplanes (the first a few minutes before midnight) and had then observed the distant flares fired by the Japanese at the outset of the attack. On all three ships there was a tendency to explain away the warning signs: the airplanes were assumed to be friendly; the flares were interpreted as star shells fired to illuminate these aircraft.

The bridge watch on *Vincennes* was first to conclude that something was amiss, and awakened Captain Riefkohl. But for some reason he was not informed of

Vincennes *(below) and* Astoria *(right),*
along with their sister ship Quincy,
formed the northern patrol group under
Vincennes's *commanding officer,*
Captain Frederick L. Riefkohl (inset).

Patterson's radio warning. A bank of rain and cloud obscured events to the south, but Riefkohl could see gun flashes and concluded that the southern patrol group had engaged an enemy force. However, he worried that this was a diversion before a main attack. (If only Captain Bode on *Chicago*, which unlike *Canberra* possessed a tactical radio, had thought to inform the northern group what kind of force he was facing.) Unsure what to do, Riefkohl ordered the three cruisers to increase speed to 15 knots and waited for something to happen.

Captain Moore reached *Quincy*'s bridge just as the excited klaxon announcing general quarters sounded through the ship. At about 0150, before he'd even had time to size up the situation, searchlights illuminated all three cruisers—*Vincennes* in front of him and *Astoria* behind.

"Fire at the ships with the searchlights on," he ordered—he had to assume they didn't belong to friendly vessels. But *Quincy*'s 8-inch guns weren't ready to go into action, and Moore impatiently barked, "Fire the main battery!" Before his guns could fire, his own ship began to take hits—first on the fantail and then on the bridge.

When general quarters sounded, Quartermaster Second Class Thomas Morris shot out of his bunk and fell to the floor (his was the second of four tiers). He had

been sleeping in his clothes, so he just pulled on his shoes and headed aft to his battle station. Out on deck it was as bright as day as searchlights bathed the ship and men ran to their stations. Morris frantically clambered up the ladder to Battle Two, where the secondary conn was located. This was a bunkerlike compartment near the top of the after superstructure. If the bridge were wiped out, it would become the command center of the ship. As Morris clapped on his telephone headset he glanced at the clock on the bulkhead. It read 0150. Then all hell broke loose outside.

Out on the hangar deck, Ensign Harris Hammersmith was climbing the silo toward the starboard catapult when one of his ship's scout planes burst into flames that soon spread to the superstructure. Undaunted, he continued climbing. The only thought in his mind was reaching his battle station, the number two scout plane. He had just reached the base of the catapult when *Quincy*'s number one plane also caught fire, spraying burning gasoline. Acting on reflex, Hammersmith let go of the ladder and dove back for the hangar deck, landing on all fours. Ignoring the pain in his hands and knees, he headed for the searchlight station just forward of the airplane catapults. But this had been shot away, so he proceeded to the nearest 5-inch gun mount—number three on the starboard side amidships—to see

if he could lend a hand.

There was nothing to do, so Hammersmith and two others crouched in front of the mount. The gun crew got off a salvo, reloaded, then fired again. The next thing he knew, a mighty blast threw him several feet into a bulkhead—and saved his life. The five-inch gun mount was a smoking wreck and the two men who had been on either side of him moments before lay dead on the deck. Yet his only injury was a small scratch on the back of one hand.

All three cruisers in the northern group were soon in serious trouble. Captain Riefkohl was still wondering why he had received no report from Admiral Crutchley, whom he still didn't realize was not with the southern patrol group, when first Japanese searchlights, then shells found *Vincennes*. By the time his big guns began flailing away, *Vincennes* was already a flaming beacon for the Japanese range finders.

Astoria, the third heavy cruiser in the northern patrol line, had been the last of the three to go to general quarters and was the last to show any signs of fight. In fact the confusion of most of her senior officers would have seemed comic in other circumstances. The one exception was her gunnery officer, Lieutenant Commander William Truesdell, who was already at the main battery director. He repeatedly asked the bridge to sound the alarm, but the officer in charge there refused. Finally, with enemy ships already firing, Truesdell took the law into his own hands and ordered the big guns to let forth. And an enlisted man, Quartermaster Third Class A. Radke, sounded the general alarm without waiting for an order to do so.

The guns' blast brought Captain William Greenman to the bridge, where he promptly ordered "Cease firing" until he could be sure their targets were enemy. So more precious moments were lost. "For God's sake give the word to commence firing!" Truesdell pleaded as more salvoes landed around the cruiser. Finally Captain Greenman gave permission for firing to be resumed.

The three American cruisers, all aflame and thus easy targets for the Japanese, soon found themselves sandwiched between two lines of enemy ships and under a relentless barrage. In many ways it is surprising they fought as well as they did. *Vincennes's* gunners managed to damage heavy cruiser *Kinugasa's* steering mechanism. (However, after several torpedo hits and more punishing shellfire—and with all his guns out of action—Captain Riefkohl would finally order abandon ship at 0230.) *Astoria's* final

(Overleaf) The Japanese cruiser Yubari *fires on* Astoria, Quincy *and* Vincennes, *all of which are outlined by Japanese searchlights.*

salvo flew over its intended target but struck Admiral Mikawa's flagship, putting *Chokai*'s forward 8-inch turret out of business.

The worst damage was inflicted on the Japanese by *Quincy*, despite her many wounds. On the badly damaged bridge, Captain Moore realized he was caught in a crossfire and, fearing he was about to ram *Vincennes*, turned sharply to starboard toward the eastern group of Japanese attackers, firing salvoes and taking torpedo hits as he charged. "We are going down between them. Give them hell!" he exhorted. Two or three of *Quincy*'s shells hit *Chokai*'s chart room, about twenty feet aft of Admiral Mikawa, killing most of the men in the room.

Then, just after 0210, another hit devastated *Quincy*'s bridge and killed almost everyone there. Captain Moore's last words to the signalman who stood at the wheel amid the flames and carnage were "Beach the ship." The signalman turned the wheel toward Savo Island, but *Quincy* had no hope of making it. She was already sinking fast from two torpedo hits on the port side. Lieutenant Commander Billings stumbled out of the flaming pilothouse with half his face shot away, but he was still able to mumble, "Everything will be okay, the ships will go down fighting," before he collapsed. (He would go down with the ship.) The final blow came at 0216, when yet another torpedo struck, apparently on the starboard side aft, and the ship began sinking fast.

T HE NEAR-MISS OF *CHOKAI*'S BRIDGE MOMENTARILY stunned Admiral Mikawa and his staff. The three American cruisers, although enveloped in flames, were returning fire with increasing accuracy when, almost in unison, their firing abruptly tapered off. One of the three (this was *Quincy*) had already developed a heavy list. Damage to the Japanese attacking force was minimal.

Mikawa now confronted a critical decision. Should he head for home or regroup and attack the transports? It was just past two in the morning. Fewer than four hours remained until daylight and an almost certain counterattack by carrier-based airplanes (he had no inkling that Admiral Fletcher had withdrawn). He would need up to two of these precious hours to reform his ships into battle formation. And he could not be sure how many enemy warships remained. Finally, at 0223, he gave the order, "All forces withdraw." Not all his subordinates agreed with this decision. Captain Mikio

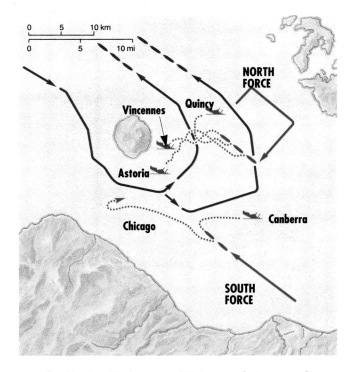

After blasting Canberra *and* Chicago, *the Japanese force broke into two lines, enveloping the north force.*

Hayakawa begged him to reconsider, but Mikawa's mind was made up. With luck his retreating force would lure the American carriers within range of Japanese shore-based aircraft, adding even greater luster to his success.

And so the Japanese passed up an opportunity to strike a potentially crippling blow at the invasion force. Mikawa had won a great victory, but it would prove to be a hollow one.

W HEN THOMAS MORRIS CAME TO HIS SENSES ON *Quincy*, it seemed as if he had awakened in hell. Battle Two was on fire; the wheel and compass— all the instruments—were gone. The last thing he remembered before passing out was seeing the man who'd been standing next to him, still wearing his headset but with his entire body in flames. Now Morris seemed to be alone in the blasted inferno. Strangely he felt no pain, but when he tried to stand, he couldn't. (In fact his left hip socket had been shattered.) He thought of his mother and his brothers and sisters back on the dairy farm. Fear and hopelessness overcame him and he began to cry. (It was a good thing his father couldn't see him now, he thought. His father didn't approve of men who cried.) And he prayed.

The Quincy *as seen from a Japanese ship, on fire and trapped in the Japanese searchlights.*
The flames on the left are Vincennes, *and* Astoria *is probably the small flash just visible to the right.*

Somehow he pulled himself together and began to crawl, using only his hands. One of his first handfalls landed in a warm, wormy stickiness. He couldn't allow himself to fully comprehend that this was a man's stomach—best not to think at all. He dragged himself out onto the deck where more flames and fallen men met his gaze. He recognized one of the bodies—a third-class signalman named Sullivan, who had been stationed on the platform above Battle Two. They had been friends. He tried to wake up his fallen comrade, but Sullivan's sleep was permanent.

Morris now found his way blocked by a gun shield—in his state a seemingly insurmountable barrier. Then he spotted a monkey rope nearby, a line with fist-sized knots in it to aid in climbing. Summoning strength he didn't know he had, he managed to pull himself up and over the barrier only to find himself dangling in thin air. Then someone called out, "Drop," which he did. A body broke his fall, and he landed softly on the roof of turret number three.

The sailor who had cushioned his fall helped lower him down to the fantail where others had gathered. There a pharmacist's mate removed all of Morris's clothes except his dungaree shirt and did what he could to dress his wounds while the ship's list increased alarmingly to

port and the stern rose out of the water. The wound was so far up his left leg that the tourniquet kept slipping into it.

Chief Bosun's Mate George Strobel sat and comforted Morris, then carried him to the port side. "I won't leave you, son," he told him, and they fell over the side together into the water. But Strobel lost his grip and Morris panicked. He felt as though he was going to go down forever, that he would be caught under the sinking ship and sucked down with her. But he clawed his way to the surface and gulped air—and Strobel was right there. Strobel pulled him over to a roll of corked net—shaped like a floating barrel—and Morris grasped onto it for dear life. Then the chief swam off to help another wounded man. On his return, he tied their two hands together with a belt draped over the floater net. Finally Morris could rest.

In the after steering engine room located just above the ship's rudder, smoke was pouring down the ventilator so fast that the three men stationed there decided to close it, but then the stale air became even less breathable. Over the headset Quartermaster Third Class Nathaniel Corwin's last communication from the bridge indicated that *Astoria* had been hit. Now Corwin had lost contact with both the bridge and Battle Two. He didn't need to be told that *Quincy* was in deep trouble.

Suddenly the cramped space went black except for the beam of light from a lone battle lantern—enough for him to see the rudder gauge. He watched as the needle went all the way to the left, then jammed—the rudder was stuck. He waited, thinking he might get a bell signal from the bridge. No bell came, so the three of them straightened out the rudder. When the ship began to heel sharply to port, they decided it was time to get out. But the hatch was red-hot from the fires on deck, and they had a hell of a time prying it open. When Corwin finally emerged onto the sloping, blood-slicked deck he slid right over the side, landing on top of someone already in the

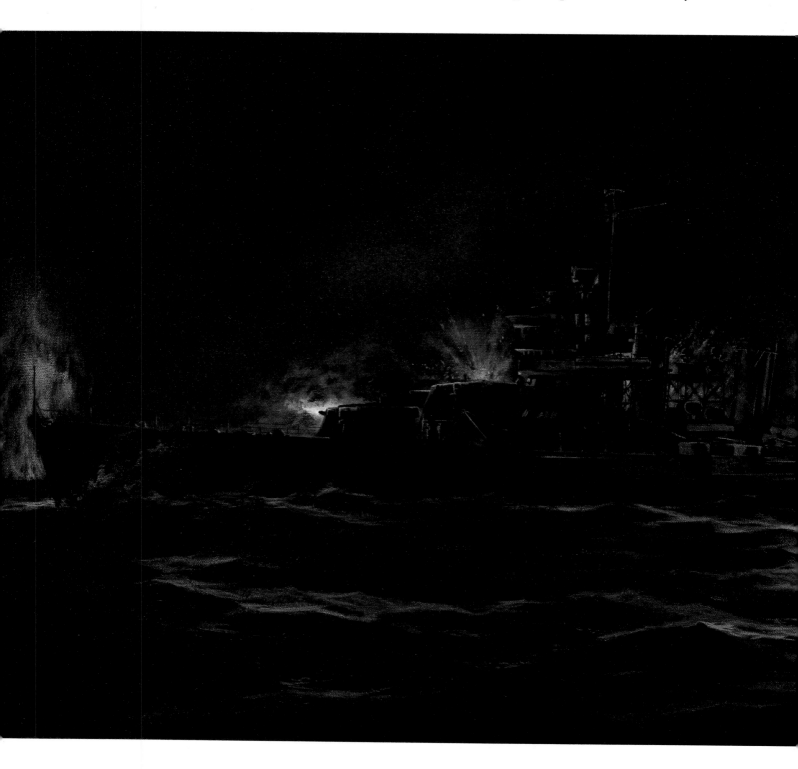

water. Then someone landed on top of him.

Many eyes watched from the water as *Quincy* sank. According to Colonel Warren P. Baker, who had been on board as a spotter for the First Marine Division artillery, "a tremendous explosion ripped through the *Quincy* as she started down, and capsizing to port, she slipped beneath the sea bow first, her stern reared high in the air with the propellers still churning." By his watch the time was 0235, less than an hour since *Chokai's* searchlights had first brought *Quincy's* officers to their senses.

The hundreds of men already in the warm oil-soaked waters contemplated the night ahead. They feared killer sharks and wondered whether the Japanese ships would return. *Vincennes* and *Astoria* still flamed brightly against the dark. The former sank about fifteen minutes after *Quincy*. *Astoria* would hang on considerably longer.

THE BATTLE HAD LONG LEFT *Canberra* and *Chicago* behind, but these first two casualties of the Japanese surprise attack were still afloat. The luckier of the two was *Chicago*, which, despite the torpedo hit to the bow was not otherwise severely damaged. She had power and could still maneuver. *Canberra*, by contrast, was a floating disaster, with her captain desperately wounded, a huge fire blazing amidships, many shell holes in her hull, and her superstructure in ruins. She was also developing a serious list to starboard.

Able Seaman Henry Hall, who had left the fore control station once the ship lost power, helped carry wounded from the bridge area—now a shambles of twisted wreckage and dead or dying men—to the forecastle deck. One injured midshipman put up a fuss, insisting that he wouldn't leave until the captain

Before she was fatally wounded, Quincy's captain had swung the cruiser out of line to starboard with guns blazing.

was tended to. But Captain Getting still refused any treatment until the other men were looked after. When Commander J. A. Walsh, the ship's executive officer, arrived on the scene, the captain was fading fast. His last order to Walsh before losing consciousness was a whispered, "Carry on."

Surgeon Lieutenant Morris had moved his medical mission to the forecastle where he worked by flashlight on those wounded that could be treated. Rain fell, heavy at times. Around him lay heads without bodies, trunks without limbs, but he kept his gaze on the living. He didn't even stop to curse when some overzealous officer yelled, "Put out those lights," as if their feeble beams outshone the raging fires that made the ship visible for many miles. One man, whose belly wall had been split open by shrapnel, remarked almost casually to everyone who passed by, "Don't tread on me guts."

As Stoker Second Class George Faulkner carried yet another wounded man to be laid out on the forecastle deck, he couldn't help reflecting that only a few days earlier this had been a favorite sunning spot for crewman "getting brown for leave." When the sun became too hot, they would seek the shadow of A turret to "spin a dit"—chat idly—or play a game of cards. Faulkner noted that the ship was listing noticeably to starboard.

He wondered how long she would last.

Able Seaman Stephen St. George, clad only in his blue turret shorts, explored much of the forward part of the ship, searching for wounded. It seemed like eons since the card game he and his mates had been playing in the Y turret handling room when the battle began. He was heading up the stairs from the wardroom (the main medical station) to the quartermaster's lobby when he encountered a man named Halliwell leaning on a sailor's shoulder. "Let us through, boys, I've only one leg," Halliwell announced cheerily. On a later trip to the wardroom, St. George found Surgeon Lieutenant Warden and the two ship's chaplains hard at work. He offered cigarettes to the living. Then, locating the officers' beer supply, he gave each of the wounded men a glass. When he offered the same to the doctor and the priests, the Roman Catholic chaplain declined—so St. George drank the good father's share.

Those who weren't helping tend the wounded dumped ammunition overboard or formed a bucket brigade to fight the fires as best they could (the ship had lost water pressure). The rain helped, but there was only so much that could be done. At one point Sub-Lieutenant Gregory decided to return to the forward control station to retrieve his officer's cap—he'd tossed it

aside to don a tin helmet during the battle. It wasn't the cap he was after so much as the gold-embroidered cap badge that he had purchased from Gieves' naval outfitters in London while taking his sub-lieutenant's course in England. (The cap badges available in Australia were stamped out of metal and not nearly so classy.) When Gregory reached his action station, however, he found only a large hole where the cap had been.

Around 0330 the destroyer *Patterson* came in along

Despite the fierce beating she had taken, Canberra *remained afloat the next morning, tended by American destroyers (*top and above*), which fought her fires and evacuated the wounded before sending her to the bottom.*

the port side forward and began to take off wounded, including a still-breathing Captain Getting, while providing pumps and fire hoses for fire-fighting. The evacuation proceeded smoothly until about 0430 when someone on *Patterson* shouted, "Out all lights!" She had sighted an enemy ship. The destroyer swiftly dropped lines and pulled away, although her captain called out, "We'll be back." Several shells flew overhead and *Patterson* returned a few salvoes before the "enemy" identified herself as *Chicago*, which soon realized her mistake. *Patterson* returned to *Canberra*'s side; then destroyer *Blue* came up and joined the relief effort.

SEVERAL MILES TO THE NORTH, THE HUNDREDS OF men still on board *Astoria* fought to save her from sinking. They battled a fire amidships so fierce that the group on the bow and the group on the stern were unaware of each other. *Vincennes*'s and *Quincy*'s survivors, meanwhile, clung to life rafts, cork nets, empty shell casings and powder containers—anything that would float. The occasional scream pierced the night as a shark attacked one of the wounded. At one point, a darkened ship—Allied or Japanese, no one knew—sliced soundlessly through their midst and then disappeared. Occasionally it rained.

When the strange ship brushed by Harris Hammersmith's crowded life raft, he clutched the .45 pistol his father had carried as an army sergeant in World War I and vowed he would never be taken prisoner. (He had heard rumors about brutal Japanese treatment of prisoners.) The gun clip was full—seven rounds—and there was one bullet already in the chamber. Eight in all. Seven rounds were for the Japanese; the eighth was for him.

Hospital Apprentice First Class John Giardino clung to two powder cans and thought about home. His wounds weren't really bothering him. He had a gash in his head, a piece of shrapnel in his shoulder and another big gash in his back, but the salt water seemed to have stopped the bleeding. His only complaint was a slight headache. But it was awfully lonely out there in the water and the darkness. "Wait till I tell my sister Carm about this," he thought. Carmella wrote him every day, and her letters meant everything to him. Suddenly he realized that he might never see his sister again.

Sometime before dawn he floated into contact with another man, who was using a sea bag for buoyancy. "Is that you, Gerry?" the man asked. "Doc?" Giardino replied. It was Merlin "Doc" Schwitters, the medical petty officer Giardino had trained under and his best friend on *Quincy*. They managed to float together for awhile. But Doc's suggestion that they both use his sea bag proved a poor one. In the confusion it filled with water and sank, and the two friends became separated. (They didn't meet again until both were safely on board the transport *American Legion*.)

When one raft became too crowded, some of the men took Fireman First Class William Montgomery and laid him on a cork net, which acted like a floating stretcher. The shrapnel wound in his leg didn't hurt too much, and he drifted in and out of consciousness, listening to the quiet talking nearby. One of the voices sounded familiar. "Is that you, Jenny?" he called out. "Yeah. Who's that?" came the reply. "The Snipe" (this was shipboard slang for a fireman). Montgomery had been the engineer on the same motor launch where Jenny—Seaman Second Class Thaddeus Janeczko—had been the "stern hook" responsible for manning the stern grappling pole when docking. "Come on up here and we'll shoot the breeze," Janeczko called out. "Well, Jenny, I can't," Montgomery replied. So Janeczko slipped out of the raft, swam over to his friend and climbed onto the net. For the rest of the night he sat there cross-legged with Montgomery's head cradled in his lap.

Near dawn help arrived in the form of *Ellet*, which had been one of the destroyers that had been guarding the transports and taken no part in the battle. As two sailors with rifles watched for sharks, the survivors, wounded men first, were lifted on board. Meanwhile the destroyer *Bagley* rescued the sailors perched on the bow and stern of the still-burning *Astoria*. Other ships later picked up survivors who had drifted out of the area of the sinkings or who had vainly attempted to paddle their life rafts to Savo. At least one life raft carrying *Quincy* survivors drifted out to sea. All the men on it would likely have died had not an American scouting plane spotted the raft several days later and dropped food, water and medical supplies. As it was, the survivors were not picked up until two weeks after *Quincy* sank.

When Thomas Morris was brought on board *Ellet*, the thing he wanted most in the world was a drink of water. But after several gulps it all came back up in a hurry—all over the officer who was holding him. (He was too ill to recognize Harris Hammersmith, who years later reminded him of this incident at a *Quincy* reunion.) After several more failed attempts to keep water down, Morris passed out and was carried to an officer's bunk below. Later he awoke in a panic to the sound of guns firing—he was sure the Japanese were back and that this time they were surely goners. (He later discovered that *Ellet* was firing on *Canberra*, which Admiral Turner had ordered scuttled or sunk if she could not get her engines started and retire under her own steam.)

Although Hammersmith was safe now, he simply couldn't get warm. (He didn't realize it, but he was undoubtedly suffering from shock.) Finally, he went down to the *Ellet*'s engine room, the hottest place on the ship. The chief engineer welcomed him and offered him a cup of coffee. When he took his first sip, he almost choked. It was half bourbon. He would later say, "It was the best god-damned drink I ever had in my life."

SOME FIRES STILL BURNED ON *CANBERRA*, BUT SHE DID not seem to be sinking. However, there was no immediate prospect of repairing the engines. So Admiral Crutchley, acting on Turner's orders, directed that she be sent to the bottom. Soon after daybreak the last of the wounded were taken off and the last officers left the ship. Then destroyer *Selfridge* moved in. But despite 263 rounds of 5-inch shells and four torpedoes, the stubborn lady refused to surrender. Destroyer *Ellet*, joined in around 0730 (this was the firing that temporarily woke Tom Morris). And it was one of *Ellet*'s torpedoes that delivered the coup de grace. At 0800, after all her surviving officers and men had been carried ashore, H.M.A.S. *Canberra* turned over to starboard and then sank by the bow.

THE NIGHT OF AUGUST 8-9 CANNOT HAVE BEEN A good one for Admiral Turner. From his flagship *McCawley*, anchored with the other transports off Beach Red, he could see the distant aircraft flares and the flashes of gunfire, so he knew a battle was raging, but could discern neither its disposition nor its result. Nonetheless, he faced a crucial decision. Admiral Fletcher's carriers had already withdrawn out of range, General Vandegrift had not yet reported on the situation on Tulagi, and at least two more days were needed to transfer all the food, fuel and equipment still on his ships to Guadalcanal. As he had told Vandegrift at their meeting the previous evening, the prudent course was for his ships to withdraw. Yet, to quote Guadalcanal historian Richard Frank, "he displayed his mettle by deciding to stay for another day

of unloading without air cover." One last time he sent a message to Admiral Fletcher requesting him to bring back his withdrawing carriers. Fletcher did not reply.

After daybreak, when Turner discovered the full extent of the defeat, he must have thought seriously about reversing his decision, but he held firm. And he was lucky. The Japanese airplanes dispatched that day expended their efforts in sinking destroyer *Jarvis*, damaged during the August 8 air raid, as it limped away to the south. (All hands were lost.) Even without this final blow, the margin of Japanese victory against a superior force was stunning: four heavy cruisers sunk against minor damage to *Chokai* and *Tenryu*. It was the worst defeat the United States had ever suffered in a surface battle. Not including those on *Jarvis*, the Allies had lost a total of 1,077 killed, with 700 wounded. Only 58 Japanese were killed and 70 wounded. Two Allied captains died during or soon after the action. Captain Samuel Moore went down with *Quincy*; Captain Frank Getting, slated for a speedy promotion to admiral, died of his wounds later that day. And Captain Howard Bode of *Chicago*, deeply humiliated by his failure to engage the enemy, subsequently committed suicide.

Although Chicago (right) *was damaged during the battle, the ship's captain, Howard Bode (below), was criticized for withdrawing. Under a cloud, he later committed suicide.*

AWN FOUND ADMIRAL MIKAWA'S FORCE SPREAD OUT in anti-aircraft formation and speeding away up the Slot. Mikawa paced the bridge and watched the sky anxiously, expecting the inevitable air attack at any second. But no planes appeared. Later in the morning he detached four heavy cruisers, *Aoba*, *Furutaka*, *Kinugasa* and *Kako* for the more distant base at Kavieng on the northwest tip of New Ireland, where they would be safer from air attack. He and the remaining ships sailed for Rabaul. However, the Japanese triumph was to be marred the next day when a lone American submarine torpedoed and sank *Kako*.

For the ordinary seamen on *Chokai* the victorious mood was laced with sadness. Thirty-four of their shipmates had died and forty-eight lay wounded. It was the first time since the start of the war that seaman Kurato Yoshiie had seen the ship's carpenters making coffins. He was one of those assigned to help load them with bodies, which proved grisly work, since many of the

dead men had been blown apart and one often had to guess which arms went with which heads and feet. The only consolation was that the men had died honorably.

In Japan news of the great victory was greeted with euphoria, and as further proof of the supremacy of the Japanese navy. (No word had yet leaked out of the disastrous defeat at the Battle of Midway.) However, Admiral Isoroku Yamamoto, the Combined Fleet commander and mastermind of the attack on Pearl Harbor, was not so pleased. He sharply questioned Admiral Mikawa's failure to attack and destroy the transports, thus failing to convert a tactical victory into a decisive strategic one. Perhaps more than any Japanese commander, Yamamoto understood that the longer the Americans were on Guadalcanal, the harder they would be to dislodge.

Even so, the Japanese had gained the advantage in the struggle for control of the Guadalcanal airfield. At dusk on August 9, the remaining warships and the

(Above) The cruiser Kako, *torpedoed by an American submarine while returning to base, was Mikawa's only major loss.*
(Below) After Turner's invasion force sailed away from Guadalcanal on August 9, 1942, the marines were on their own.

transports weighed their anchors and steamed out of the body of water that had just earned its future name, Iron Bottom Sound. Admiral Turner had unloaded little heavy equipment and only a small portion of the embarked food supplies. For the next eleven days, as the marines rushed to complete the airstrip, the under-equipped forces on Guadalcanal and Tulagi would be without air cover or naval support. As Admiral King would say when he learned of the Savo Island debacle, "The whole future then seemed unpredictable."

WAKING
THE GHOSTS
OF SAVO

FIFTY YEARS AFTER ONE OF
WORLD WAR II'S FIERCEST SEA BATTLES,
WE REDISCOVER THE LOST SHIPS OF
GUADALCANAL'S IRON BOTTOM SOUND.

WE ARRIVED AT GUADALCANAL IN LATE JULY 1992 with only three weeks to locate and photograph the key wrecks from each battle. Fortunately, our ship, the *Laney Chouest* (a Louisiana mudboat designed for operating around drilling rigs in the Gulf of Mexico), was perfect for the job. She was equipped with a sophisticated dynamic-positioning system that allowed her to stay in one spot even in strong winds and currents— essential for close work around a sunken wreck. On board we had a sophisticated deep-towed sonar (which

(Left) Our research ship, the Laney Chouest, *off Guadalcanal. (Above) The three-man submarine* Sea Cliff, *which worked together with the remotely operated vehicle* Scorpio, *begins a descent to the floor of the sound.*

(Top) Laney Chouest's large open stern and heavy cranes made her ideal for storing and launching Sea Cliff, at center, our side-scan sonar, right, and Scorpio, on the far right. (Above) We used this deep-towed sonar device to locate ships for Scorpio and Sea Cliff to explore and photograph.

we would use when in a search phase), *Scorpio*, a remotely operated camera vehicle that would handle still photography, and *Sea Cliff*, a three-man submarine almost identical to *Alvin*, in which we had explored the *Titanic*.

Scorpio and *Sea Cliff* are both owned by the U.S. Navy, which had decided to support our expedition as a way of helping to mark the fiftieth anniversary of the Guadalcanal invasion. *Sea Cliff* would be piloted by a team of navy submariners who joined a hand-picked group of veterans from my previous expeditions.

Two historical consultants—Richard Frank, author of *Guadalcanal*, the definitive book on the whole campaign, and Charles Haberlein of the Naval Historical Center in Washington, D.C., an expert on warships and naval guns—were on hand to identify what we discovered.

This was midwinter in the southern hemisphere, but the weather was hot—in the nineties—relieved only by the occasional tropical downpour. And when the weather wasn't getting us down, we were plagued by recurring problems with our equipment. When one of our two vehicles was working, the other one always seemed to need fixing.

Our two prime targets from the Battle of Savo Island were the Australian heavy cruiser *Canberra* and the American heavy cruiser *Quincy*. *Canberra* was the only Australian ship sunk in Guadalcanal waters. She was also the vessel that bore the brunt of the first phase of the Japanese attack. And *Quincy*, according to the Japanese who sank her, put up the bravest fight of the three cruisers in the northern group, all of which were sunk during the battle's second phase.

However, we had failed to locate either of these ships during our preliminary expedition in 1991. And without them, we would be unable to do justice to the first major battle fought in Iron Bottom Sound.

But on the first day, the wreck of *Canberra* came out of nowhere as we retraced the very last search line we had run the previous year—just to orient ourselves and make sure there were no gaps between our search areas. There she was, large as life on the sonar screen. Don't ask me how we could have missed her in 1991. Technology is imperfect at the best of times.

Canberra survivor Bert Warne sat with us in the control room as we piloted *Scorpio* over the wreck of his former ship—an emotional experience for him and us. At one point he reluctantly agreed to take the controls and steer the vehicle. Under his guidance *Scorpio* passed

(Above) Scorpio *enters the water.* (Left) Scorpio *shown ready for launching. Remotely operated by means of a fiber-optic cable,* Scorpio *took most of our still photographs and could also send back video images of the wrecks as she explored them.*

(*Top left*) Sea Cliff *in her hangar aboard the* Laney Chouest *just prior to a dive.* (*Bottom left*) *The navy divers and our three-man crew prepare to roll out the sub.* (*Right*) *After* Sea Cliff *hits the water and all internal systems check out, the divers release her tether. When she surfaces, they attach the tether and the sub is winched back on board, as is shown below.*

over the spot where he had been stationed when the battle began—the shell room below Y turret—and the hatch through which he had emerged onto deck after his nightmare passage through the smoke-filled lower decks.

Quincy also fell to us early, several days into the expedition. The sonar identified a target that was the right size and only about a mile from where historians said the ship went down, although technical problems with both *Scorpio* and *Sea Cliff* prevented us from getting a visual look for several more days. When we did, we saw that the bow was gone forward of number one turret, her remaining guns pointed crazily, and the bridge was a disaster area.

These two ships, *Canberra* and *Quincy*, suffered horribly during the brief twenty-two minutes of the Battle of Savo Island. Now they lie in peace, fitting monuments to the men who fought and died on them.

CANBERRA

CRIPPLED IN THE OPENING MOMENTS OF
THE BATTLE OF SAVO ISLAND, THE AUSTRALIAN HEAVY CRUISER
HUNG ON UNTIL MORNING, WHEN ALLIED GUNFIRE
DELIBERATELY SENT HER TO THE BOTTOM.

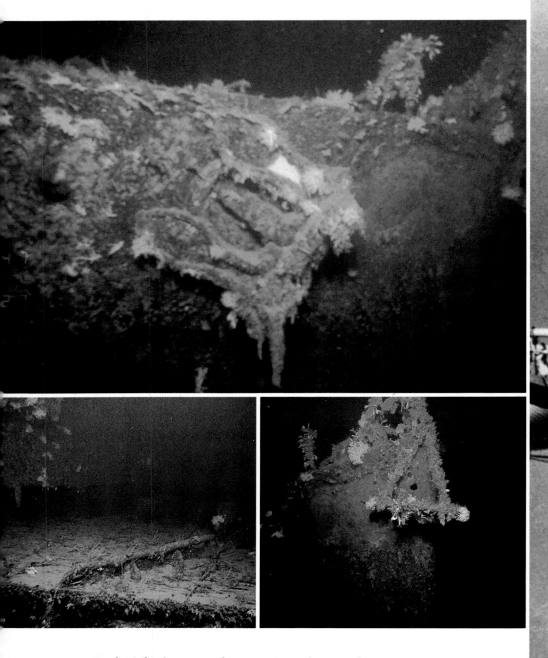

*(Right) This bow view of H.M.A.S. Canberra in her prime conveys
a sense of her size and power. (Top) One of her starboard anchors is still
readily recognizable half a century later. (Above left) Canberra's
breakwater sits in front of "A" turret. (Above right) This stanchion,
perhaps a part of her railing, now hangs over the bow.*

(Left) Canberra at Wellington, New Zealand, shortly before leaving for Guadalcanal. (Above left) Fire may have weakened the plating of her starboard side superstructure; time and salt water have done the rest.

(Top right) Canberra's forward-most turret, equipped with 8-inch guns (see inset) that are still trained out as if ready to fire. (Above) Her starboard set of quadruple torpedo tubes is badly damaged but still identifiable from this picture (right) of a similar ship.

U.S.S. Quincy

Quincy's lost bow and collapsed rear deck are a testament to the severe bombardment she suffered.

1. Remnants of flagstaff.

2. Aft-most 1.1 inch anti-aircraft guns.

3. Collapsed deck.

4. Tilted aft superstructure.

5. Wreckage of hangar for scout planes.

6. Supports for aircraft catapults.

7. Uptakes for smokestacks.

8. Five-inch guns.

9. Broken mast.

10. Blast shield, upended on sinking.

11. Burst 8-inch gun.

12. Jammed gun.

13. Severed bow.

QUINCY

Sunk in the second stage of the Battle of Savo Island,
Quincy put up a fierce struggle before being torpedoed.

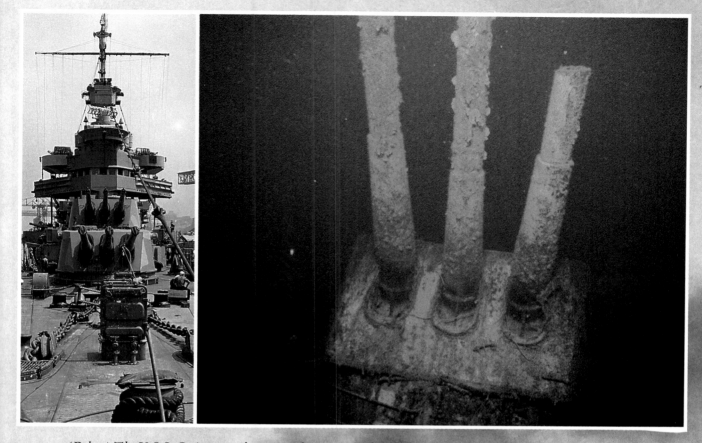

(Below) The U.S.S. Quincy *as she appeared in May 1942, at the New York Navy Yard, just before transferring to the Pacific Fleet. The metal overhang that shielded the windows on* her bridge is still recognizable (opposite top). (Above left and right) Quincy's forward 8-inch guns as they looked then, and her upper turret now with one barrel shattered, probably by a barrel explosion during battle.

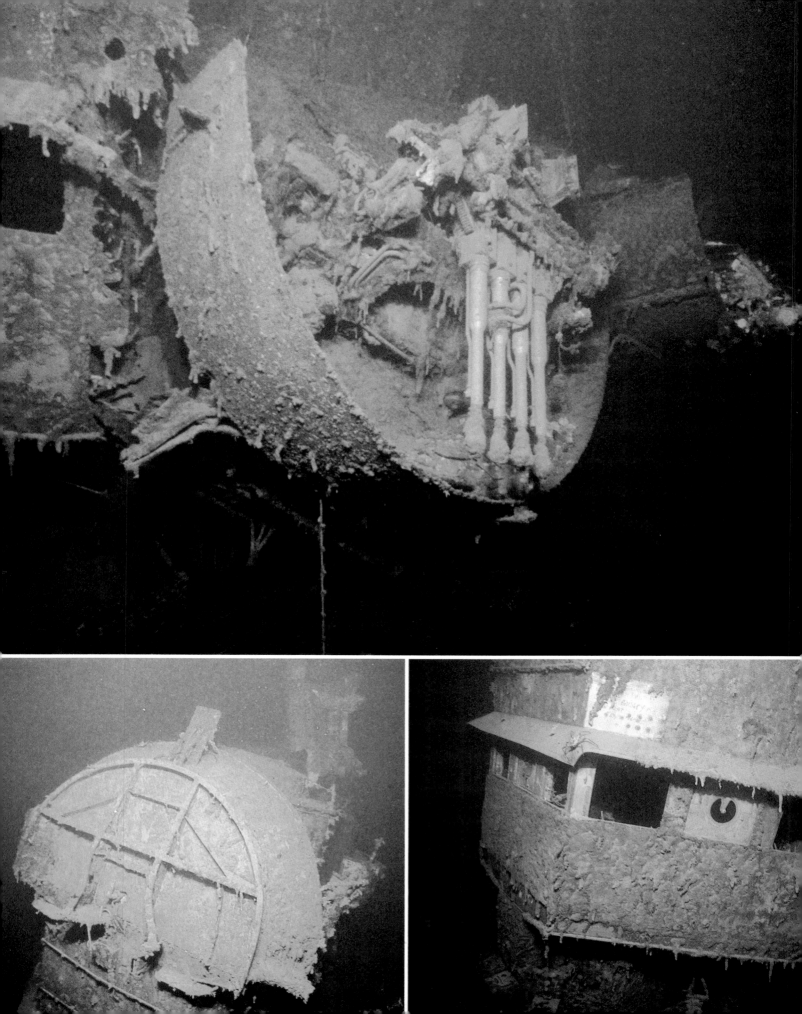

Quincy's bridge (below) and as it is today (opposite bottom right). The bridge took a nearly direct hit during the battle, which inflicted serious damage and killed many of the crew stationed there. (Opposite) The 1.1-inch anti-aircraft battery above the chart house has dropped downward, while (opposite bottom left) the distinctive "bird bath"

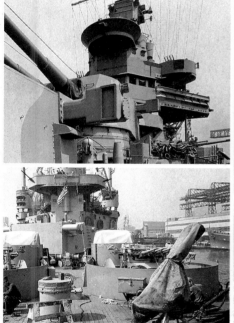

atop her bridge, actually a shield intended to protect her range finder, was probably forced up by water as the ship sank. Quincy's stern area (above) took some of the first hits, and the deck there has caved inward (top right), tilting her two aft anti-aircraft batteries at odd angles and (right) leaving the after turret now high above the deck.

(Left) This 5-inch, dual purpose gun is the same gun shown in the foreground in this dockside picture of Quincy (above).

(Top) The upside-down tub here is one of Quincy's anti-aircraft fire control stations. Its port side counterpart is just visible at the very top of the picture above.

(Left) Quincy seen from astern in May of 1942. (Top right) Her stern today. The dents in its underside may be the result of the hull imploding on sinking. (Inset) The flagstaff on the stern. (Bottom right) Quincy's outboard starboard propeller, now half-buried in the mud of Iron Bottom Sound. The inboard propeller has disappeared, perhaps lost on impact with the bottom.

CHAPTER FOUR

TOE TO TOE

August – November, 1942

MARTIN CLEMENS MOTIONED HIS MEN TO a halt, then bent down to put on the pair of black dress oxfords sent him by another coastwatcher on Guadalcanal. The shoes were too small and looked completely out of place with his torn shirt, dirty shorts and battered bush hat, but Clemens was determined to put on the best show possible. Then he formed up his small company of native constables—all that remained of the British law on Guadalcanal—into two neat rows, their ancient rifles sloped smartly on bare shoulders, the Union Jack flapping in the breeze. Finally, with a small white dog at his heels, he marched his men out of the jungle fringe and onto the beach. At the other end of the stretch of white coral sand, a marine sentry raised his gun and

Heavy American artillery bombards the Japanese in this Guadalcanal painting by Dwight Shepler.

(Above) Martin Clemens poses with his scouts. Once he had crossed over American lines, Clemens went to work as an intelligence officer on Vandegrift's staff (right). (Left) Jacob Vouza, the most famous of Clemens's scouts, was captured by the Japanese, bayoneted and left for dead. Miraculously, he managed to drag himself back to the American lines, and he eventually recovered from his wounds.

aimed. If he were going to die, thought Clemens, this would be the moment. Instead the young marine held his fire and stared at the strange platoon advancing toward him. As it moved closer, he lowered the gun and waved them forward.

Since March, Clemens had been the only representative of the British Crown on Guadalcanal— and one of the few Europeans left on the island. Since June 20, when the Japanese first landed troops and built a wharf at Lunga Point, he had observed their activities and radioed reports, moving his base whenever things got too hot, always wondering when the enemy would finally catch up with him.

Now, as he approached the American lines he had visions of a hot bath, a good meal and a comfortable bed. He didn't realize he had simply moved from being an isolated man on the run to a member of a garrison under siege.

The day Clemens marched up to the astonished sentry was August 15, 1942, less than a week after Admiral Turner's ships had departed. In that time the marines had worked frantically to complete the airfield—aided immeasurably by abandoned Japanese equipment— and to prepare against the expected enemy counter attack. Fortunately for them, the Japanese air fleet based at Rabaul had been severely depleted by its raids on the landing force and had been quiet until August 14, when it launched its first bombing raid since the landings. But the marines still had no airplanes, little artillery and too few men to repel a determined Japanese landing. (It was assumed at this point that the Japanese would attempt an amphibious assault similar to the one that had put the Americans on Guadalcanal in the first place.) Without airplanes—promised soon, but still not forthcoming—and without naval or air support, the marines were sitting ducks.

Given this situation, the August 15 arrival of four ships bearing aviation gas, bombs and ammunition was a good omen. Apart from proving that it was possible to keep the forces on Guadalcanal supplied, it presaged the arrival of aircraft for the newly anointed Henderson Field (named after marine pilot Major Lofton Henderson, a squadron commander who had been killed at the Battle of Midway). In fact the first planes and pilots appeared five days later on August 20—nineteen Wildcat fighters and twelve Dauntless dive bombers of Marine Air Group 23.

Clemens, meanwhile, was appointed to General Vandegrift's intelligence staff, to which he proved an invaluable addition. He organized his native scouts to patrol the island and report on enemy activity. Over the next several months they would constitute a vital source of information as the marines struggled to maintain and consolidate their fragile hold on the airstrip.

DURING THE DAYS FOLLOWING THE GUADALCANAL invasion, the strategic minds at Japanese Imperial General Headquarters had been busy contemplating their countermove. But planning was hampered by confusion as to the strength and true intentions of the Americans. This confusion grew out of inadequate intelligence and out of distrust and faulty communication between the army and navy, whose enduring rivalry created many problems over the course of the war. The navy had still not admitted to the army the extent of its losses at the Battle of Midway, knowledge that would certainly have encouraged army strategists to view the American offensive as something more than a "reconnaissance in force," which was their initial assessment. But even as Japanese strategists began to accept that the Americans were present in numbers that suggested a determination to stay, they tended to underrate their adversary. What's more, they were still preoccupied with New Guinea, where the big push over the mountains to Port Moresby was about to begin. The result of this muddled situation was a piecemeal approach to dislodging the enemy from Guadalcanal. The first piece was a woefully inadequate one.

Just before midnight on August 18, a convoy of Japanese destroyers entered Iron Bottom Sound and swept silently past Lunga to Taivu Point, about twenty-two miles east of the airstrip. The Japanese officer in overall command of the operation, Rear Admiral Raizo Tanaka, would soon become a master in the art of night naval reinforcement. But this was the first Japanese attempt to land troops on the enemy-held island and he worried that the odds were stacked against this advance force of six destroyers under Captain Torajiro Sato. (Tanaka himself had assumed direct command of a larger, slower convoy scheduled to arrive several days later.) Tanaka needn't have been concerned. The Americans had no naval vessels or planes to send against the Japanese and Captain Sato met no enemy resistance. By 1 A.M. on August 19 slightly more than nine hundred troops had safely moved ashore.

This was an advance force led by Colonel Kiyono Ichiki, a hotheaded veteran of the war in China. He was determined to throw the Americans off the island without waiting for the remainder of his force traveling on Tanaka's slower convoy. Ichiki marched his men westward along the coast until dawn, advancing about nine miles, then melted into the jungle to wait for nightfall.

Until now General Vandegrift's mostly untested troops on Guadalcanal had engaged in only a few sporadic skirmishes with the scattered and disorganized Japanese forces they had taken by surprise during the initial landings. (The most ominous of these encounters had occurred on August 12, when the division intelligence officer, Lieutenant Colonel Frank Goettge, led a night patrol to capture a group of Japanese who apparently wanted to surrender a few miles west of the American lines. Goettge was killed and the patrol virtually wiped out.) But American intelligence had warned Vandegrift to expect a serious attempt by the Japanese to retake the island as early as August 20. Reports from Clemens's scouts on Guadalcanal

suggested the enemy attack would come from the east, a prediction lent credibility when three Japanese destroyers bombarded Tulagi on the morning of August 19 (Tanaka had detailed them to distract attention from Ichiki's landing area).

Around noon on the nineteenth, a reconnaissance patrol under Captain Charles Brush encountered an advance patrol sent by Ichiki to establish a communications post near the lagoon at the mouth of Alligator Creek (also known as the Ilu River), about one mile east of the airfield. Ichiki's men apparently shared their commander's cocky overconfidence, for they took few precautions, walked into an ambush and were almost all killed. From their fresh army uniforms and the documents they carried, it was clear that new troops had arrived on the island. But Vandegrift still had no inkling

of their numbers, or of where they would attack.

Vandegrift reinforced his defensive line along the west bank of Alligator Creek and waited, but not for long. Colonel Ichiki was a man in a hurry. Undeterred by the loss of a complete patrol, he moved up his troops and ordered an attack without even bothering to reconnoiter the enemy's position. Soon after midnight on August 21, the Japanese stormed across the sandbar at the lagoon's mouth. The well-positioned marines on the west bank remorselessly mowed down the attackers, but a few made it past the barbed wire and fought the defenders hand to hand. A timely counterattack wiped out this small group of Japanese, and although Ichiki threw his reserve into the battle, the marine line held. Before dawn the Japanese commander withdrew most of his troops to a coconut grove about two hundred yards east of the lagoon. Sporadic firing across the lagoon continued through the night.

Ichiki's best option was retreat, but he chose to stand his ground, seemingly unable to believe the Americans could beat him. This gave the marines the opportunity to outflank and entrap his forces. By afternoon the surviving Japanese troops were all pinned down in the small triangle formed by the lagoon and the sea. Colonel Ichiki finally accepted that he had suffered a humiliating defeat, burned the regimental colors and committed suicide, as did many of his officers. But his men fought on. Some died in a hopeless attempt to fend off tanks without anti-tank guns. Others who took the only escape route, which was to sea, were shot or drowned. Only one unwounded Japanese soldier was captured.

The day after the battle, war correspondent Richard Tregaskis described the scene: "The stench of the bodies strewn along Hell Point [where the west bank of the lagoon meets the sandbar] and across the spit was strong. Many of them lay at the water's edge, and were already puffed and glossy, like shiny sausages. Some of the bodies had been partially buried by wave-washed sand;

(Opposite) Colonel Kiyono Ichiki. (Above) Many of Ichiki's men died as they charged over the sandbar across the mouth of Alligator Creek. (Below left) Others were caught in a nearby grove. (Below right) American hospital corpsmen help a wounded Japanese, one of the few under Ichiki's command to survive the battle.

you might see a grotesque, bloated head or twisted torso sprouting from the beach. . . . But that carnage was a pale painting, compared to the scene in the grove across the spit. That was a macabre nightmare. We saw groups of Jap bodies torn apart by our artillery fire, their remains fried by the blast of shells. We saw machine-gun nests which had been blasted and their crews shredded by canister fire from our tanks. The tread tracks of one of our tanks ran directly over five squashed bodies, in the center of which was a broken machine gun on a flattened bipod." Japanese losses in dead and wounded were staggering—almost eight hundred of the nine hundred in Colonel Ichiki's detachment. For the marines, who had suffered slightly more than a hundred casualties, including forty-four dead, the Battle of Alligator Creek was a lopsided victory, but it gave a grim foretaste of the fighting to come.

(Above) Japanese veterans and relatives still return to Guadalcanal to search for the remains of comrades and family members. Here bones recovered from the *Alligator Creek battle undergo ceremonial cremation. (Below) Alligator Creek, showing Henderson Field's runway in the immediate background.*

WHILE COLONEL ICHIKI'S MEN WERE BEING needlessly sacrificed at the mouth of Alligator Creek, Rear Admiral Tanaka was approaching Guadalcanal in a slow convoy carrying the remainder of Ichiki's detachment. The troop transports carried about eleven hundred troops along with supplies and munitions—ample resources, it was believed, for the colonel to prevail against what was still thought to be a small occupying force. Unlike the first fast destroyer run, Tanaka's convoy was backed by the vast resources of the Japanese Combined Fleet, including three aircraft carriers. More important to the Japanese admirals than reinforcing Guadalcanal was the prospect of luring the American aircraft carriers into a battle.

On the American side, the sortie of the Combined Fleet was suspected but could not be confirmed. Analysis of Japanese radio traffic was inconclusive. Admiral Fletcher and his own considerable task force of three aircraft carriers lurked southeast of the island, covering the supply route to Guadalcanal and staying just out of range of airplanes from the nearest Japanese land base at Rabaul. Each side sent out reconnaissance planes to search for any sign of the other. The carrier battle to come would largely be determined by who found whom first—and who was quicker to act on the information.

On the afternoon of August 23, with neither side having yet found an enemy carrier, Admiral Tanaka's convoy was roughly 250 miles north of Guadalcanal. He was not a happy man. For one thing, he had learned that enemy planes were now operating from the Guadalcanal airfield, giving the Americans local air supremacy. For another, one of his destroyers, sent ahead to Guadalcanal to attack a small American convoy, had itself been attacked by carrier-based planes. Now to make matters worse, enemy flying boats had found his ships and were shadowing him through the steady rain. An attack by enemy aircraft seemed certain the next day. Clearly he would need air cover to complete his mission successfully. As if all this weren't enough, he had also received conflicting orders. In the morning the Eighth Fleet Commander, Admiral Mikawa, had ordered him to turn north and out of harm's way. Now the Eleventh Air Fleet, also based at Rabaul, ordered him to carry out the landing the next day. Tanaka demurred, explaining that some of his ships were simply too slow to reach the island in time. As he turned north once again, he wondered whether the crucial air support would be forthcoming when he needed it.

(Above) Rear Admiral Raizo Tanaka, the tenacious maestro of the "Tokyo Express."

On August 24, while Tanaka's reinforcement convoy once again moved hesitantly toward Guadalcanal, the small Japanese carrier *Ryujo,* positioned to the south of the bulk of the Japanese forces, all well north of Guadalcanal, launched an air raid on Henderson Field. In the event no American carriers were found that morning, *Ryujo's* airplanes would provide cover for Admiral Tanaka. Unfortunately for *Ryujo,* her planes were tangling with the nascent Henderson Field air force, when planes from the U.S.S. *Saratoga* (Admiral Fletcher's flagship) found the Japanese carrier and attacked. She was badly damaged and later sank.

To the south, the Japanese had finally located the American carriers *Enterprise* and *Saratoga* and sent an

(Above) A Japanese bomb scores a hit on the U.S.S. Enterprise. During the Battle of the Eastern Solomons, Japanese aircraft succeeded in putting the carrier out of action. The next day, Tanaka's flagship, Jintsu (right), was badly damaged by American bombs. The large Japanese carriers Shokaku (below) and Zuikaku were undamaged, but suffered serious losses in planes and air crew.

attacking force to get them. (The third American carrier, *Wasp*, had inopportunely been sent southward to refuel.) The Americans, meanwhile, spotted the Japanese fleet carriers, *Shokaku* and *Zuikaku*, but with most American aircraft already committed to attacking *Ryujo*, failed to mount an effective strike. *Enterprise* bore the brunt of the Japanese air attack, taking several bomb hits that put holes in her flight deck, damaged one of her airplane elevators and temporarily cost her steering control. But a second wave of Japanese planes miscalculated their position and missed her by a few miles, her auxiliary steering was successfully engaged and she was able to withdraw to fight another day. This narrow escape helped establish her reputation as a lucky ship.

Admiral Tanaka was close enough to *Ryujo* to see the "gigantic pillar of smoke and flame" on the eastern horizon that signaled her demise. That night, however, he heard better news. Two enemy carriers had been attacked and were on fire (in fact only *Enterprise* had been damaged). Once again he was ordered to proceed to Guadalcanal and land the troops. But he had "grave doubts about this slow convoy's chances of reaching its goal," he later wrote. "I had a feeling that the next day would be fateful for my ships." He was right.

Early morning of August 25 found Tanaka 150 miles north of Guadalcanal, busy signaling orders to his ships concerning the planned landings. Without warning, enemy planes broke through the clouds and attacked before effective anti-aircraft fire could be mounted. Great fountains of water shot up around Tanaka's flagship, the light cruiser *Jintsu*. At least one bomb scored a direct hit on the forecastle between the two forward guns, penetrating the ship's innards and wiping out the radio room and its crew. The blast knocked Tanaka unconscious. When he came to, the forecastle was on fire and the larger of his two transports, *Kinryu Maru*, was sinking. As the destroyer *Mutsuki* came alongside the transport and began taking off survivors, three enemy B-17s appeared and dropped bombs. *Mutsuki* took several direct hits and sank soon after.

Tanaka now received permission to limp for home. When he had needed air cover, the Combined Fleet had been unavailable to provide it. And so the second attempt to bring major reinforcements to Guadalcanal ended in failure. As Tanaka later wrote, "My worst fears for this operation had come to be realized."

As for the larger carrier battle, it brought little glory to either side. Both commanding admirals behaved tentatively. Weather and communications problems foiled several attacks, and golden opportunities were missed. What came to be called the Battle of the Eastern Solomons was an American victory. The Japanese lost an aircraft carrier and seventy-five airplanes; the Americans escaped with one damaged carrier and the loss of twenty-

five airplanes. Although the margin of victory was not decisive, the lopsided airplane loss ratio in favor of the Americans marked a trend that would ultimately be Japan's undoing. Unlike the Americans, the Japanese could not replace planes and trained pilots fast enough to make up for their losses. As Admiral Yamamoto had predicted, in a war of attrition, the Americans would ultimately be the winners.

WITH THE INITIAL SPARRING OVER, THE MONTH OF September would prove to be an even bloodier one on and around Guadalcanal. The first couple of weeks established a basic pattern that would persist for the next two and half months. By night, when it was too hazardous for American fliers to operate from Henderson Field, the Japanese destroyers dashed into Iron Bottom Sound, unloaded supplies and reinforcements, then sprinted back up the Slot before the Henderson Field fliers could catch them. These nocturnal visits became so regular that the Americans dubbed them the Tokyo Express. By day, bolstered by local air support, American supply ships were able to keep the island's lifeline intact and gradually build up the defenders' arsenal. As historian Richard Frank has written, it

Newly landed Japanese troops make their way along the shore of Guadalcanal.

was "a sort of mutual siege," with each side gearing up for the big land battle that would break the impasse. The Japanese, although still slow to shift their attention from the campaign to capture Port Moresby, were determined to take the airfield. The marines were determined to hold it.

Henderson Field's code name was Cactus, and the

(Above) Henderson Field
mechanics at work. (Left) Pilots
lounge in front of the Japanese-
built Pagoda. (Below) The crest of
the First Marine Air Wing, the
"Cactus Air Force." (Right)
U.S. Army P-39 fighters. (Below
left and right) To minimize the
effectiveness of Japanese attacks,

planes on the ground were widely
dispersed and personnel took
refuge in bomb shelters.
(Far right) The aftermath of a
Japanese air raid.

fliers on Guadalcanal soon came to be known as the Cactus Air Force. The planes and pilots were largely marine, but many navy airmen participated with distinction, including the Wildcats of VF-5 and a number of dive-bomber and torpedo-bomber squadrons. (The one Army fighter squadron involved was the 67th, whose slow-moving P-39s were most useful for attacking enemy ground troops.) Despite these fliers' efforts, Henderson Field took endless punishment, and the almost daily bombing made life miserable for the American troops. Practically every night at least one Japanese plane interrupted sleep with bombs or flares. The marines, who seem to have had a nickname for everything, called these nocturnal pests "Louie the Louse" (a single-engined floatplane) and "Washing-machine Charlie" (a twin-engined bomber that made a kind of clanking sound).

Several members of the Cactus Air Force became aces, including the rakish Joe Foss (above), a captain in a marine Wildcat squadron who was awarded the Congressional Medal of Honor.

Robert Ferguson, a member of the 67th, kept a diary in which he described one of the first daytime air raids he experienced: "We watched 21 bombers come over, a beautiful formation, aiming right at the field. Most bombs missed the runway and killed a lot of men. They may have been trying to hit the Marines who have been fighting for days along the Tenaru River.... It is a terrible feeling that cannot be described, just sitting there in a foxhole watching the bombs dropping all around you. It's that helpless kind of situation, and the Nips are really giving us hell here now."

Ferguson went on to describe the food in unvarnished terms: "We eat two meals a day with a Marine artillery unit. . . . The meals are small and the rations short. A lot of supplies were lost during the landing or didn't get ashore and we are eating mostly captured food—Jap rice that is full of weevils in the morning and Jap rice with weevils and some kind of canned fruit mixed in with it in the afternoon. Or is it the other way

(cont'd on page 110)

Even in Guadalcanal's harsh environment, life settled into a set routine.

Four words constantly pop up in all accounts of the life of the American troops on Guadalcanal: heat, mud, mosquitoes and bombs. Each day around noon a black flag shot up the Henderson Field flagpole and everyone ran for foxholes and dugout air-raid shelters.

But nearly two-thirds of the men on Guadalcanal were knocked out of duty by health problems, far more than suffered from bombs or bullets. The two thin meals a day never satisfied and soon the hearty young men who'd been so eager to see combat turned into gaunt, sunburned zombies, their uniforms in tatters, their socks gone, their boots held together by pieces of string. Disease was rampant—foot ailments, diarrhea, dysentery and above all, malaria.

An effective anti-malarial drug called Atabrine was available, but most refused to take the medicine, falsely believing it would permanently turn their skins yellow and—even worse—render them impotent. As sickness, stress and pure exhaustion took their toll many became hollow men, staring blankly from enlarged pupils, not responding when spoken to.

The food rations—a combination of captured Japanese stores, dehydrated potatoes, powdered eggs, and Spam prepared in

(cont'd overleaf)

(Above) A "surrender ticket." Combining helpful suggestions on how to surrender with an eye-catching visual, these leaflets were scattered over the American lines by Japanese aircraft.

(Left) The marine encampment in the coconut plantation near Henderson Field flooded after heavy rains. (Top right) The taking of grisly souvenirs was not uncommon on Guadalcanal. (Above) A chaplain conducts a funeral service. (Right) Americans and Melanesians relaxing with canned refreshment.

every conceivable manner—had an unfortunate side-effect on the members of the Cactus Air Force: at the reduced pressures of high altitudes they produced horribly painful intestinal gas. The almost nightly air raids meant the flyers got little relief from the daily stress of battle. Only one out of the first twelve bomber skippers was actually able to walk to the plane that eventually carried him away from Henderson Field. Six weeks was reckoned to be the maximum length of time flying crews could function well in such conditions. All stayed much longer. According to Richard Frank, "at Guadalcanal the circumstances were probably the worst any American airmen faced for a prolonged period during the war."

Yet despite the grim reality, life went on. A lively trade developed in Japanese souvenirs—swords, flags, personal diaries—not to mention the spoils of rampant petty thievery (at one point an entire case of Scotch

went missing from General Roy Geiger's personal stock). In late September, after the Battle of Bloody Ridge, when it became clear the First Marines were in for the long haul, the "great Guadalcanal housing boom" saw all manner of makeshift shacks and lean-tos spring up to replace the now patched and leaking tent city that was put up after the initial landings. The marines invented a slang term for almost everything, although their conversation increasingly consisted of muttered strings of profanities. Each scrap of news and above all every letter from home was devoured hungrily.

Despite all these privations, the American troops were far better off than the badly supplied Japanese, thousands of whom died of disease or starvation.

(Above) As the Americans' stay on Guadalcanal lengthened, life became more settled, and sturdier structures replaced the tent shelters (far left) of the early months. But for the most part, amenities remained primitive, with the island's rivers functioning as the only place to bathe (left and right).

(Left) Marine gunners manning a portable 75mm gun. (Above) Edson's Ridge as it looks today. (Right) Merritt Edson (in later life) and (opposite left) some of his raiders. (Opposite top and right) Edson's Ridge after the battle.

I have never felt so helpless."

Instead of his neat coordinated attack, only the few troops that had actually reached the attack point south of Edson's Ridge made contact. A few fierce forays tested the marines' right flank, which lay across a low swampy area between the southern point of the ridge and the Lunga. A frustrated Kawaguchi was forced to postpone the big push until the following night.

By nightfall on September 13, the Japanese general's bedraggled main force had regrouped. During the day Colonel Edson had pulled back slightly to present a different defensive position so as to disorient the enemy, but he remained thin on the ground. Shortly after sunset flares dropped by Japanese planes and shouts of "*Totsugeki!*" (Charge!) announced the Japanese attack. Then wave after wave of screaming soldiers brandishing swords and rifles charged the weary marine lines, gradually forcing them to fall back along the ridge. More than once the Japanese came close to breaking through, but sheer guts and tenacity combined with the marine artillery held them off. After midnight about three hundred marines made what looked like a last stand on the

final knoll between the attackers and Henderson Field. Somehow the line held and gradually the tide turned.

There was much individual bravery, extraordinary discipline under fire, "but the soul of the defense this night," writes Richard Frank, "was Merritt Edson. A scant ten or twenty yards behind the firing line—his clothes were pierced at the collar and at the waist by bullets—exhorting the steadfast and excoriating those few who wavered: 'Go back where you came from. The only thing they've got that you haven't is guts.' "

While Kawaguchi's legions stormed the ridge, only one of the other two prongs of his attack managed to engage the Americans. This was the eastern wing, which was repulsed after a hard fight. As many as eight hundred Japanese soldiers died in these two assaults, compared to fewer than a hundred Americans. But in some ways the worst ordeal for Kawaguchi's men was the withdrawal through the jungle. Exhausted from the fight, their rations gone, the retreating soldiers carried wounded comrades on makeshift litters across the incredibly difficult terrain. Many men died from their wounds or from starvation.

And so the first serious Japanese attempt to retake Guadalcanal came to an inglorious close. Edson's Raiders had saved the airstrip. With each passing day, as more planes and supplies arrived, the Americans' ability to hold onto their precious toehold in the Solomons improved. The best boost to the morale of the long-suffering marines was the arrival on September 18 of more than four thousand men of the Seventh Marines with supporting artillery. But the serious fighting was far from over.

THE NEWS OF GENERAL KAWAGUCHI'S DEFEAT WAS greeted at Imperial General Headquarters with disbelief and dismay. (Characteristically, the army blamed the failure on a lack of navy air and surface support; the navy ascribed it to army incompetence.) But it marked an important strategic shift. Henceforth the recapture of Guadalcanal would be the focal point of all offensive action in the South Pacific. New Guinea was on hold until Guadalcanal and its airfield were back in Japanese hands. Large numbers of fresh troops were earmarked for a decisive battle. They would be under the command of Lieutenant General Harukichi Hyakutake of the Seventeenth Army, Kawaguchi's superior officer.

On Guadalcanal the marines reinforced their defenses. The Tokyo Express again swept down the Slot almost nightly. In late September and again in early October, Japanese and American troops tangled near the Matanikau River to the west of the airfield. In the fighting the Japanese lost their forward positions on the river's east bank. Since these had been designated as assembly points and artillery emplacements for the coming October offensive, the loss threw Hyakutake's plans into disarray. Meanwhile Japanese air attacks, which had tailed off following the defeat at Bloody Ridge, resumed. But they concentrated on night bombing runs that interrupted sleep more than airfield operations. The strengthened Cactus Air Force was now more than a match for anything the enemy could sortie by day.

On October 9, General Hyakutake himself landed to take personal command of a force that numbered more than twenty thousand men, all of them positioned west of the airfield (the tiny remaining contingent to the east had been wiped out by an expedition of marines from Tulagi). On the same day Admiral Turner left Noumea, the American naval headquarters on New Caledonia, with more reinforcements for Guadalcanal.

(Above) Rear Admiral Norman Scott, pictured here as a captain.

These were the first army troops assigned to the island—2,800 members of the Americal Division, so-called because it was originally assigned for duty on New Caledonia. Three task forces sailed in support of Turner's convoy, one with the express purpose of disrupting enemy naval activities around Guadalcanal. This was a group of two heavy and two light cruisers escorted by five destroyers, under the command of Rear Admiral Norman Scott.

The fifty-three-year-old Scott was a career navy man who had been the executive officer on a ship sunk by a German U-boat in 1917. He began World War II working for Admiral King in Washington and had only returned to active sea command in June. (He had commanded the ships patrolling the eastern entrance to Iron Bottom Sound during the Battle of Savo Island, and had not been involved in the action.) Determined to prove that the Americans could match the Japanese at naval night action and derail the Tokyo Express, he had rehearsed night firing with his ships and issued a clear battle plan. The stage was now set for the second major naval battle to be fought in the waters immediate to Guadalcanal, the engagement known as the Battle of Cape Esperance.

The heavy cruiser San Francisco *served as Scott's flagship during the Battle of Cape Esperance.*

On the afternoon of October 11, with Turner's convoy still a day from Guadalcanal, Admiral Scott received reports of two enemy cruisers and six destroyers steaming down the Slot. The cruisers were in fact seaplane carriers being used for a particularly crucial Tokyo Express run carrying artillery—including four howitzers—ammunition and more troops for General Hyakutake, all to be unloaded at the western end of the island (the Japanese had given up on landing troops east of the airfield). Scott, who had been waiting safely south of Guadalcanal for just such an opportunity, immediately raced north to intercept this group, unaware that a second and more powerful Japanese force was charging in behind the reinforcement convoy. This consisted of three heavy cruisers and two destroyers, whose job was to bomb Henderson Field while the reinforcement group was unloading. In command was Rear Admiral Aritomo Goto aboard the heavy cruiser *Aoba*.

Scott's task force approached Guadalcanal about two hours before midnight, made a wide swing around the island's western end, then formed into a single battle column—three destroyers followed by his four cruisers followed by two destroyers—and set a course just east of north that would keep it to the west of Savo.

Scott's plan was to patrol back and forth across the southwestern entrance to Iron Bottom Sound and thereby intercept the enemy. His scout planes reported several enemy ships to the east off the northwest coast of Guadalcanal, but he decided this couldn't be the cruiser force sighted earlier, so he stuck to his plan.

At 2325, just as the lead destroyer in Scott's column neared the Savo Island end of his first patrol line, the radars on two of his cruisers, *Helena* and *Salt Lake City*, both received contacts from a group of ships almost sixteen miles distant and galloping in at 30 knots from the northwest. As the contacts became clearer there could be little question this was an enemy force, but before either ship could report this information, Admiral Scott ordered the American column to turn left and reverse course, retracing its steps on a southwest heading. This coincidence convinced his captains that he, too, had contacted the Japanese and was maneuvering for tactical advantage. In fact his ship had not picked up the enemy.

Admiral Goto had been handed opportunity on a silver platter, but he couldn't seize it. Japanese ships as yet possessed no radar, and Goto was completely unaware of the Americans' presence. Worse yet, he was unprepared to encounter an enemy force. Nighttime in

Guadalcanal waters ordinarily belonged to the Japanese, and Goto assumed that, as usual, the Americans would not attempt to take on the Tokyo Express. His ships weren't even at general quarters. His cruisers were armed for shore bombardment, not surface action. It was Savo Island in reverse: Japanese complacency versus American alertness.

But that alertness was being undermined by confusion. Because of a communication breakdown on Scott's flagship, *San Francisco*—first of the four cruisers in the American line—she turned left simultaneously with the lead destroyer. The perplexed captain of *Boise*, the cruiser immediately behind the flagship, concluded he had better follow the admiral rather than the destroyers. And the remaining ships in the line followed *Boise*, creating a double turn and two American columns. This left the three van destroyers racing to catch up to the head of the column they were supposed to be leading. Thus when Admiral Scott finally received the first contact reports of the enemy formation—now off to his starboard side—he doubted their authenticity. Weren't these his own destroyers? He hesitated to issue the order to commence fire. Radar was a newfangled technology, and he for one was not convinced of its reliability or accuracy. Meanwhile Goto bore down on the confused American double column, still unaware of its existence.

Finally *San Francisco*'s gunnery control radar picked up a contact less than three miles away. Still Scott hesitated to fire. His captains, more convinced than he of the enemy's presence, were reluctant to commence the action before their admiral, even though he had given them the authority to do so. The priceless advantage of surprise was about to be lost. Someone on *Helena* reported "Ships visible to the naked eye," and in her radar room an ensign who had been watching the radar blips move ever closer could stand the suspense no longer. "What are we going to do, board them?" he heatedly asked the navigator. Moments later his captain took matters into his own hands and opened fire with his 6-inch guns. The time was 1146.

Despite Scott's hesitation and the inadvertent splitting of his battle formation into two columns, the American admiral found himself in an excellent position. In the parlance of naval tacticians, he had "crossed the T." His forces formed the top of an imaginary T, with the Japanese as the stem. Thus his guns were in a position to bear on the enemy, whereas only their forward guns could do so. Even better, on *Aoba*, Admiral Goto persisted in believing the enemy silhouettes belonged to the Japanese reinforcement group that had preceded him down the Slot. He turned to starboard and flashed recognition signals. In answer shells tore into his bridge, killing many and mortally wounding him. As his ship took a terrible pounding, the cruiser *Furutaka* charged to relieve him and was herself badly damaged. Meanwhile his third cruiser, *Kinugasa,* turned to port and thus avoided damage in the battle's first phase.

At one point Admiral Scott ordered all his ships to cease firing, fearing that he was attacking his own destroyers. (In fact both *Farenholt* and *Duncan,* two of his lead destroyers, were caught in the crossfire between the opposing forces and were hit by American shells.) But most of Scott's commanders ignored his order to hold fire and continued punishing *Aoba* and *Furutaka*. From the Japanese point of view, the American gunfire seldom slackened, and with two of three cruisers limping badly, they began to withdraw.

Near midnight Scott regrouped his forces and gave chase to the retreating Japanese, whose fight was far from spent. The still-undamaged *Kinugasa* rounded on the pursuers and launched torpedoes that narrowly missed *Helena* and *Boise*. The Japanese cruiser then homed in on *Boise*, embracing her with straddling salvoes before pinpointing the range. At about 1210 the first shell hit, jamming the light cruiser's number one turret. Soon the forward part of the ship was ablaze and more than a hundred men had died at their stations. As *Boise* turned and raced away from the scene, she was saved from sinking by the seawater that poured through the shell holes in her hull. This doused the fire in her holds before the main powder magazines ignited.

At 1216 the battle was over. Of the three Japanese cruisers, *Kinugasa* escaped most lightly, having taken a few hits from *Salt Lake City* while she was covering *Boise*'s retirement. More badly damaged, *Aoba* was nonetheless able to accompany *Kinugasa* northward, carrying her dying admiral. *Furutaka*, however, soon lost power and sank. (The Japanese also lost one destroyer in the night action and two more in its daylight aftermath.) Despite the damage to *Boise* and the loss of one destroyer (*Duncan*), the Americans got off lightly. But perhaps their most important victory was a psychological one. They had proved they could beat the Japanese at night fighting.

They had not proved, however, that they could derail the Tokyo Express. While the Battle of Cape Esperance was raging, the reinforcement group quietly unloaded its guns and troops and headed back up the Slot. Those guns would soon prove a mighty irritant to General Vandegrift and his men.

ANY EUPHORIA AT ADMIRAL SCOTT'S NAVAL VICTORY and the arrival that morning of Turner's convoy carrying the 164th Infantry Regiment of the Americal Division was dispelled the following night, which saw the worst bombardment of Henderson Field during the entire campaign. The fireworks began just before midnight, when the battleships *Haruna* and *Kongo* entered the sound and launched a deadly rain of 14-inch shells at their target. Lieutenant H. Christian Merillat, a marine public relations officer, dove into the nearest shelter as the bombardment began. "There I huddled with about a dozen others," he recorded in his diary, "at the bottom of a quaking heap, while we went through the worst bombardment we have yet had. The shelter shook as if it was set in jelly. . . . No sooner did we get back to our tents than relays of planes again started to come over. The first bomber-load caught me on the way to the dugout. I dived into an open hole and thought my

end had come. They hit close." Throughout the night and into the morning the shells and bombs were joined by "Pistol Pete," the nickname for the newly arrived Japanese field guns.

Rear Admiral Tanaka was the commander of the destroyer escort for the two battleships that gave Henderson Field such a pounding that night and observed from a distance its effect. "Fires and explosions from the 36cm shell hits on the airfield set off enemy planes, fuel dumps, and ammunition storage places . . . the whole spectacle making the Ryogoku fireworks display seem like mere child's play. The night's pitch dark was transformed by fire into the brightest day. Spontaneous cries and shouts of excitement ran throughout our ships." The next morning the airfield was pocked with craters and most of the airplanes were unusable.

During the bombardment the Tokyo Express successfully landed one of it largest troop contingents of the entire campaign—4,500 men. The build-up was underway for yet another attempt to wrest Henderson Field from the stubborn Americans. (But despite the punishment to the airfield, the Cactus Air Force was back in operation the next day, managing to sink three of the retiring transports.) On October 15, Admiral Chester Nimitz, supreme Allied commander in the Pacific,

The Kyusyu Maru *was one of three transports that were run aground and easily bombed and burnt on October 15.*

penned this grim assessment: "It now appears that we are unable to control the sea in the Guadalcanal area. Thus our supply of the position will only be done at great expense to us. The situation is not hopeless, but it is certainly critical."

Nimitz could do little to alter the practical reality—with the invasion of North Africa imminent, American military resources were already stretched to the limit—but he could do something to change the psychological situation. For some time he had been concerned about the fitness of the chief of the South Pacific forces, Rear Admiral Robert Ghormley, whose hands-off leadership style had contributed to the near debacle of the August landings when Admiral Fletcher withdrew his aircraft carriers two days early. Now Nimitz decided to replace Ghormley with a more aggressive commander, Vice Admiral William Halsey. Aggressive he was. He had helped strike the first offensive blow of the war in the Pacific, leading the carrier task force that sent the first American bombers over Tokyo in the daring Doolittle Raid. Before the Battle of the Santa Cruz Islands in late October, he would issue one simple order to his admirals: "Attack, repeat, attack!" Upon being informed of his new appointment, Halsey is reputed to have said, "Jesus Christ and General Jackson! This is the hottest potato they ever handed me!" It was, and he didn't drop it. For the rest of the Guadalcanal campaign, the men on the island never doubted that Halsey was backing them to the hilt.

During the week following the October 14 bombardment, almost every night was a sleepless one on Guadalcanal as bombers pounded the airstrip. And almost every night another load of Japanese troops came ashore. Only a handful of American planes were able to take to the air each day and only a trickle of supplies—including precious aviation gas—managed to sneak through. Finally General Hyakutake was ready.

Once again the Japanese underestimated American strength. They thought the airstrip had about ten thousand defenders, when in fact there were twice that many. (The total Japanese force on the island now numbered more than twenty thousand.) Once again they failed to factor in fully the difficulties of the terrain, planning another simultaneous three-pronged attack that again proved impossible to coordinate. It was scheduled for October 22, but its main thrust, this time just south of Bloody Ridge, had to be postponed to the following

Feeling that more aggressive leadership was needed in the South Pacific, Admiral Chester Nimitz (left) appointed William Halsey (right) as commander of the South Pacific forces.

(Above) The October 26, 1942, Battle of the Santa Cruz Islands, east of Guadalcanal, was the first test of Halsey's skill.

night. Once again the jungle had worn down the attackers before they had to fight. The defenders, now reinforced with fresh troops and better entrenched, did the rest. Japanese losses were staggering. The so-called Battle for Henderson Field cost the Americans fewer than a hundred killed; the Japanese lost well over two thousand and possibly many more.

This third vicious land battle was still raging when on October 26 another carrier engagement took place in the waters east of Guadalcanal. If the Battle for Henderson Field was in some respects a replay of Bloody Ridge, the Battle of the Santa Cruz Islands was in some ways a replay of the late August Battle of the Eastern

Solomons. Both sides had moved major naval forces into the area to provide support for their respective attempts to reinforce their soldiers on Guadalcanal. And two American aircraft carrier task forces again faced off against the several elements of the Japanese Combined Fleet, including two fleet carriers and two light carriers.

Each side simultaneously found the other's flattops and simultaneously launched air strikes (the opposing airplane flotillas actually passed within visual range of each other). This time *Enterprise* was even luckier than during the Battle of the Eastern Solomons. It was hidden in a squall and dodged the initial attack completely, although it was damaged later. Meanwhile the other

(Below left) Planes warm up on the deck of the Japanese carrier Shokaku. *Like the Battle of the Eastern Solomons, Santa Cruz pitted ships against planes. Casualties included the American carrier* Hornet *(below and below right), sunk by the Japanese.*

American carrier, *Hornet*, was stopped by bomb and torpedo attacks and sank after efforts at salvage proved futile. And the new battleship *South Dakota* was superficially damaged. This time, however, the Japanese got off more lightly than the Americans. They lost no ships, but the fleet carrier *Zuikaku*, light carrier *Zuiho*, and heavy cruiser *Chikuma* were all put out of action. Aircraft losses were more equal than in the earlier carrier battle, helping to tilt the overall tactical balance in Japan's favor. But the beating it had taken prompted the Combined Fleet to retire to its base at Truk Island to lick its wounds while the two battered flattops returned to Japan for repairs. And although the Americans were now down to a single limping aircraft carrier in the South Pacific—the nine-lived "Big E"—they had won precious time for General Vandegrift. That soft-spoken Virginian had more battles to fight. And the waters of Iron Bottom Sound had not yet finished collecting their store of wrecked ships.

IN LATE OCTOBER AND EARLY NOVEMBER, THE Japanese and Americans resembled two punch-drunk boxers entering the late and decisive rounds of a championship bout, each groping for the elusive knockout blow. The Japanese, despite the failure of their second major attempt to capture the airfield, thought they had their opponent on the ropes. They believed—erroneously—that during the Battle of the Santa Cruz Islands they had sunk four aircraft carriers and a battleship, thereby hobbling American naval power in the South Pacific. Sensing victory, they threw fresh resources into the struggle. The Americans, wondering if the Japanese would ever stop coming, continued to feed men and airplanes to the island. They had invested so much in holding Guadalcanal that to lose it now would be devastating to morale and to their overall efforts in the Pacific. President Roosevelt himself ordered that "every possible weapon" be assigned to holding the island, even as Operation Torch, the Allied invasion of North Africa, was about to commence.

As both sides geared up for the decisive round, the marines embarked on serious land offensives for the first time since the early August landings. The larger of these advanced west of the Matanikau River, pushing back the exhausted remnants of General Hyakutake's troops. To the east, near Koli Point, a second marine group took on a freshly landed Japanese force and eventually chased it into the jungle and away from the action for several

weeks. The Americans seemed to have the Japanese on the run when, on November 12, General Vandegrift abruptly recalled both prongs of these advances. Coastwatchers and radio intelligence predicted a big Japanese push the night of November 13. He wanted to be ready.

The Japanese had briefly flirted with the idea of establishing a second staging point to the east of Henderson Field, but eventually decided to concentrate their forces to the west and build up manpower and supplies there. Keeping their troops fed and armed was proving a logistical nightmare despite the frequent fast-destroyer runs of the Tokyo Express. A destroyer's speed was counterbalanced by its limited transport capacity. With so many troops now on the island it was impossible to keep them properly supplied. Nonetheless, formidable resources were being gathered for this third offensive.

Vandegrift's information was accurate. The Japanese planned a huge landing for the night of November 13, backed up by a powerful naval force. They would embark 7,000 soldiers, large quantities of munitions and supplies for 30,000 men for twenty days—long enough to achieve the much-delayed but inevitable victory.

The Japanese still held their most powerful ships—the huge new battlewagons *Yamato* and *Musashi*—in reserve, but the Americans had thrown every available warship in their South Pacific fleet into the twin tasks of reinforcing Guadalcanal and preventing the expected November 13 landings. Two American convoys bearing 5,500 troops along with crucial supplies approached from the south, supported at a distance by a task force built around the damaged but operational aircraft carrier *Enterprise*, the Americans' lone serviceable flattop. Escorting *Enterprise* were two of the most dangerous battleships in the United States Navy, *Washington* and *South Dakota*.

General Vandegrift needed all the help he could get. Although he now boasted twenty-four thousand combat troops on Guadalcanal, many had been on the island since the initial landings and most were worn down by long weeks of inadequate rations, too little sleep, battle wounds and tropical diseases—above all malaria and dysentery (on both sides malaria accounted for more casualties than battle wounds). Martin Clemens was still waiting for that hot bath.

The most decisive naval battle of the entire campaign was about to begin.

In the October push for Henderson Field, a Japanese tank force was knocked out by marine anti-tank guns at the mouth of the Matanikau River.

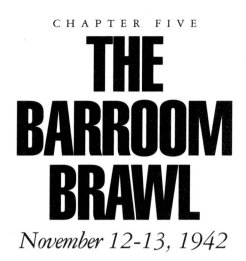

CHAPTER FIVE

THE BARROOM BRAWL

November 12-13, 1942

O N THE MORNING OF NOVEMBER 12, 1942, Lieutenant (Junior Grade) Michiharu Shinya stood on the open bridge of destroyer *Akatsuki*, bracing against the stiff breeze. At 24 knots the wind cut through his crisp khaki uniform, even though the sky above was a brilliant blue and the waves flashed and glittered with sunlight. The powerful Japanese task force that churned relentlessly southward from the Japanese base at Truk Island toward the eastern Solomons made an impressive sight: light cruiser *Nagara* and a bevy of destroyers formed a protective ring around the two *Kongo* class battleships, *Kirishima* and flagship *Hiei*. That night the two battlewagons were scheduled to deliver a punishing pounding to the Guadalcanal airstrip, immobilizing the enemy air force so that the planned landings on November 13 would take place unopposed. Then, finally, Shinya and his shipmates were to head home for long overdue shore leave. He could almost taste the fresh ice cream.

His reverie was broken when a signal flag snapped up *Hiei*'s mast, its message an unwelcome one: "Enemy plane sighted." And indeed, in the distance ahead he

An American destroyer, all guns blazing, passes behind the Japanese flagship Hiei *at the height of the action during the first night of the Naval Battle of Guadalcanal.*

could just make out the American B-17. Two Zero fighters riding shotgun above the Japanese ships immediately raced to the attack, but the enemy plane turned and disappeared over the blue horizon. Its crew had seen all they needed to.

The appearance of the enemy aircraft only increased the tension level of the task force commander, Rear Admiral Hiroaki Abe. He already had misgivings about his mission, a close copy of the October 13-14 bombardment that had so devastated Henderson Field. Now any chance of surprise was gone. Surely the Americans would not permit a Japanese raiding force to fire unopposed a second time. Well, in the event he was attacked, he would not be caught napping like his old friend Admiral Goto, killed one month earlier during the Battle of Cape Esperance. And if intelligence reports were accurate, the American convoy currently off Lunga Point was no match for his two battleships. Even though they had been built back in World War I they would overpower American cruisers. Besides, if the enemy acted according to form, the American transports and their escorting warships would be gone by dusk, leaving the enemy airstrip at the mercy of his 14-inch guns.

REAR ADMIRAL KELLY TURNER KNEW ABOUT ADMIRAL Abe's task force, but he had more immediate problems. Since dawn, his heavily escorted convoy had been unloading troops and heavy field artillery to bolster the Guadalcanal garrison for the expected Japanese offensive. Now, shortly after one in the afternoon, another timely report from coastwatcher Paul Mason on Bougainville alerted him to a Japanese air raid from Rabaul. Immediately he ordered the disembarkation suspended and got all his ships underway so as to decrease their chances of being hit.

Just after 2 P.M., sixteen Bettys, supported by thirty Zeros, swept over the ridge of Florida Island and split into two attack groups. Turner was by now a master at dodging air attacks and he deftly parried this one, offering his transports' broadsides as bait to lure the first Japanese group into a premature attack. No sooner were these enemy planes committed than his ships turned away, leaving only the narrow sterns as targets. The torpedoes all missed. At the same time, fighters from Henderson Field took on the other Japanese group. When it was all over, most of the enemy planes had been shot down before they

(Right) Lieutenant Michiharu Shinya was the torpedo officer aboard the destroyer Akatsuki *(top left), part of the escort for the Japanese battleships* Hiei *(middle left) and* Kirishima *(bottom left, on the left), whose mission was to bombard Guadalcanal.*

could score. However one flaming Betty crashed into the after superstructure of heavy cruiser *San Francisco*, demolishing a 20-mm anti-aircraft battery and knocking out the after fire control radar while killing twenty-four men and wounding forty-five others. And friendly fire disabled destroyer *Buchanan*'s torpedo tubes, killing five and wounding seven. But the transports were soon back at the work of unloading. Turner was determined to be on his way home by the time night fell.

AT 1530 ADMIRAL ABE'S FORCE RENDEZVOUSED WITH five more destroyers under Rear Admiral Tamotsu Takama. Abe sent these ships four miles ahead of his main body to form an advance guard—two destroyers in column to port, three destroyers to starboard. Meanwhile the main body formed an arrowhead shape with light cruiser *Nagara* at the arrow's point, followed by the battleships *Hiei* and *Kirishima* at intervals of approximately 2,000 yards. Three destroyers fanned out to either side of *Nagara*. (This complicated sailing formation spread out on either side of his capital ships was intended to prevent surprise by enemy submarines.) When the force approached Guadalcanal, Abe planned to send Admiral Takama's advance guard ahead to sweep Iron Bottom Sound for enemy vessels.

ADMIRAL TURNER FACED A DIFFICULT DILEMMA. He did not know whether the Japanese task force speeding in from the north was aimed at Henderson Field or would attack his transports as they retired to the south. Unless he divided his assets, he would have to leave one or the other undefended. Yet even as an unbroken unit his warships would face a superior force that included, according to reconnaissance reports, at least two battleships, possibly as many as six cruisers, and ten to twelve destroyers. To his credit, Turner gambled that the Japanese were bent on bombarding the airfield and detached all but a tiny escort to protect it. His empty transports would sail home with only three destroyers (one the damaged *Buchanan*) and two ancient minesweepers. Turner believed it was a risk that had to be taken.

Turner handed command of the five cruisers and eight destroyers that he hoped would confront the Japanese to Rear Admiral Daniel Callaghan aboard heavy cruiser *San Francisco*. The silver-haired Callaghan, whose movie-star good looks had gained him the

(*Above*) *Rear Admiral Daniel Callaghan (here a captain) was picked by Admiral Turner to lead the force opposing the Japanese.* (*Below*) *This photograph of Callaghan's flagship,* San Francisco, *shows the damage done to her after fire control area on November 12.*

(Below) The light cruiser Atlanta *was Admiral Norman Scott's flagship. Leading the battle formation was the destroyer* Cushing *(top inset), while another group of destroyers, including (bottom inset) the destroyer* Barton, *brought up the rear.*

nickname "Handsome Dan," was, in the words of naval historian Samuel Eliot Morison, "austere, modest, deeply religious; a hard-working and conscientious officer-wwho possessed the high personal regard of his fellows and the love of his men." These personal qualities aside, Callaghan was not the obvious choice to take command of this crucial and dangerous mission. Some historians have argued that Turner should have given the reins to Rear Admiral Norman Scott, the victor of Cape Esperance. Instead Scott was assigned the job of second-in-command, with no real role unless Callaghan were knocked out of the action.

Callaghan, though technically senior to Admiral Scott by a few days, was as yet unseasoned by battle. Scott had been fighting at sea for six months; Callaghan's active sea duty as an admiral had begun less than two weeks earlier (before then he'd served as Admiral Ghormley's chief of staff). Perhaps most important, Admiral Scott had recently fought and won a night battle against the Japanese. He was thus better prepared to face the psychological as well as the tactical challenges of this most difficult type of naval action. But there is no evidence that the modest Scott questioned Turner's decision.

Darkness had fallen as Admiral Callaghan's force escorted Admiral Turner and his transports out the eastern exit of the sound. Then, as Turner set a southeast course for the American naval base at Espíritu Santo, Callaghan organized his ships into a single-line battle formation much like the one Scott had used at Cape Esperance. Destroyers *Cushing*, *Laffey*, *Sterett* and *O'Bannon* took the van; cruisers *Atlanta*, *San Francisco*, *Portland*,

Helena and *Juneau* formed the center; and destroyers *Aaron Ward, Barton, Monssen* and *Fletcher* brought up the rear. Hindsight highlights two serious problems with this disposition. First, it denied the more experienced Scott any tactical independence. Second, it failed to take advantage of the Americans' most notable technological advantage over the Japanese, their radar. (As at Cape Esperance, the Japanese still possessed no radar at all.)

At the Battle of Cape Esperance, the first ship to detect the onrushing Japanese was light cruiser *Helena*, recently fitted with SG radar. This was the most advanced radar in use on American naval vessels, and it was far superior to the more primitive SC radar on most of Callaghan's ships. SC radar was notoriously unreliable and frequently made false contacts. SG radar had a finer resolution and was better able to distinguish surface targets from nearby land masses. But it seems that neither Scott nor Callaghan fully understood the priceless advantage they possessed—not surprising given how fresh the technology was and how little experience American commanders had with it. This helps explain, but does not excuse, the fact that neither man chose to fly his flag from a ship equipped with the new radar. Equally unfortunate, Callaghan failed to make good use of the ships that were. The only van destroyer fitted with an SG set was *O'Bannon*, but she was placed fourth in line. *Portland, Helena* and *Juneau*, the three cruisers with SG radar, followed behind *Atlanta* and *San Francisco*, the two cruisers without it.

Midnight passed as Callaghan's ships filed one by one back through the eastern entrance to Iron Bottom Sound and headed west along the Guadalcanal coastline. Throughout the American fleet a feeling of high-strung anticipation prevailed. Even those who didn't officially know a battle was coming had heard the scuttlebutt or could read the tension in the air.

Commander Tameichi Hara, captain of the destroyer Amatsukaze, *rightly worried that the Japanese formation sailing to bombard Henderson Field had become hopelessly confused.*

COMMANDER TAMEICHI HARA aboard destroyer *Amatsukaze* (second in the line of three destroyers off *Nagara's* port quarter) simply couldn't understand what Rear Admiral Abe was thinking. Since an hour before sunset they had been steaming south in heavy rain that often reduced visibility to almost nothing. Then, just after midnight, with the advance squadron destroyers in danger of running blind into Savo Island, the admiral had ordered the fleet to reverse course and reduce speed to 12 knots. (If the bad weather continued he would have to abandon his mission altogether.) Now Abe had ordered his ships to turn around yet again. He had received radio reports from Guadalcanal that the weather there was clearing. The bombardment of Henderson Field would proceed as planned. Yet during all this time the commanding admiral had done nothing to simplify his complex battle formation.

After hours of high-speed steaming, much of it in zero visibility, then two abrupt course changes, Commander Hara was sure this formation must be in considerable disarray. He was right. The five destroyers of the advance guard now actually trailed the main body. At 0046, when the admiral ordered this "advance" unit to conduct the planned sweep into Iron Bottom Sound to scout for enemy ships, the squadron fell into further confusion. Three destroyers ended up still trailing the main body; two (*Yudachi* and *Harusame*) found themselves slightly ahead and off *Nagara's* starboard bow. The planned sweep never took place.

At 0125 Admiral Abe's force sighted signal lights from Japanese posts on Cape Esperance and he swung his ships left onto a southeast course that would take them into the sound south of Savo. Speed was increased to 18 knots. Not realizing that his advance guard hadn't swept, he had good reason to believe the way was clear. The last sighting of enemy ships off Lunga Point had been shortly after sunset, more than six hours earlier. And his latest communication from observers on Guadalcanal reported no surface ships and no air cover over the sound. It looked as though he was in luck, that once again the enemy had disappeared with the onset of darkness. At 0130 he ordered, "Gun battle. Target airfield." On the two battleships, the young sailors in the handling rooms immediately leapt to their ammunition hoists and began loading the 14-inch bombardment shells. The main body of the Japanese force was now entering Iron Bottom Sound on a course just south of east.

ON THE DIMLY LIT BRIDGE OF *ATLANTA*, LIEUTENANT Stewart Moredock felt like something of a fifth wheel. As Admiral Scott's operations officer, he knew as much as his boss did about the expected enemy attack that night. He had only been in the job a few weeks and had been astonished to discover the degree to which the Allies were reading the enemy's radio traffic. During the Battle of Cape Esperance, he had served as junior gunnery officer on board the cruiser *Boise*, his view of the war limited to what he could see through his director sights. But with *Boise* badly damaged and heading home for repairs, he'd been transferred to the admiral's staff. Suddenly his view of the conflict was as broad as the Pacific. That day he had plotted the latest intelligence information and discussed it with Scott. He knew the enemy was on its way and in considerable force. But now all he could do was watch and wait.

A few feet away from Moredock, Admiral Scott and Captain Samuel Jenkins exchanged a few words too soft to overhear, then walked back into the flag plot to stare one more time at the chart. (The head of the American column was now passing Lunga Point heading slightly north of west—on almost a reciprocal course with the approaching Japanese.) Crackling over the TBS radio came the voices of the other ships.

Admiral Scott's junior aide, Stewart Moredock, shown here in pre-war dress uniform.

TBS (Talk Between Ships) was a recent innovation and a far from perfect system—a single frequency for all ships and for both incoming and outgoing messages. Frequently one message was drowned out by another transmitted simultaneously. In the heat of battle, this could contribute to serious tactical confusion.

At the head of the line of thirteen American ships, *Cushing*'s skipper, Lieutenant Commander Edward "Butch" Parker, contemplated his situation. He'd been in tight spots before. In January 1942, while commanding one of four old "four-piper" destroyers that had attempted to break up the Japanese landings in Borneo, he had led a night charge through a ring of enemy warships to attack landing craft, sinking five and damaging several others. He had also distinguished himself at Bali and in the Battle of the Java Sea, earning two Navy Crosses and a Silver Star for his exploits in a losing struggle against the Japanese juggernaut. Yes, he had seen some tight spots, but this looked like the tightest so far. He was new to his vessel, hadn't even found time to meet all the crew and here he was leading a column of warships into battle against an unseen and superior force.

At 0127, as Parker tried to make his eyes pierce the darkness ahead of him, *Helena* chimed in on the TBS frequency, announcing enemy ships "bearing 310, distance 31,900 yards." The enemy was just north of west and just over 18 miles from a ship in the center of the American column—therefore only about 15 miles from him—but his radar plot reported no contacts.

As at the Battle of Cape Esperance, the light cruiser *Helena* had made first contact with its SG radar set. Once again a Japanese force had been spotted before it even guessed an American force was moving to meet it. Once again, an American advantage was being frittered away, for Admiral Callaghan did not have a clear picture of the developing situation. He knew only what he could hear over the TBS frequency, which soon became jammed as other ships chimed in with queries and fresh radar reports. An enemy force was approaching, but the radio garble made tactical analysis extremely difficult. Callaghan was unsure of who was where, and so he hesitated.

As soon as Admiral Callaghan received *Helena*'s first contact report, he ordered a course change to starboard, new heading 310. He was turning his column directly toward the reported position of the Japanese fleet, presumably to close the range before opening fire. (Hindsight suggests Callaghan would have been wiser to hug the Guadalcanal shore, which would have masked his ships from the Japanese lookouts, but he probably feared this would unduly restrict his sailing room.) The range was in fact closing rapidly as the opposing forces approached each other at a combined speed of nearly 40 knots. A few minutes after *Helena*'s first report, she radioed Callaghan that the enemy ships were now 26,000 yards away. This put the Japanese about fifteen miles from the center of his column; his lead destroyers were much closer. And American radar had so far failed to detect the lead Japanese destroyers *Yudachi* and *Harusame*, well out in front of the main body. In fact, a collision between the two formations was imminent.

No one will ever know what Admiral Callaghan was thinking as he briefly pondered his next move. But it appears clear he planned to maneuver for advantage against an enemy formation he believed was still more than fourteen miles to the west. This would help explain his next order: "Column right to 000," due north. If the Japanese were still as far away as Callaghan thought, this right turn would have caused his column to pass in front of the enemy force in a rough but effective crossing of the T that would allow him to bring all his guns to bear at a range of three or four miles.

A few minutes after Callaghan issued the order to turn due north, *Helena* reported new radar contacts that must have given the admiral a jolt—four ships two miles westward, much closer than her previous reports led him to expect. Incredulous, Callaghan asked *Helena* to repeat the message and she confirmed the distance. How had the enemy ships closed in so quickly? he must have wondered. Or was this a different force entirely? Was the contact real or phantom? *Helena*'s report, if accurate, is as inexplicable today as it must have seemed to the American admiral in the blackness of the November 13 night. The four ships in a line "fan-shaped like cruising disposition" could only have been part of the main body of the Japanese force, but nothing we know of Japanese movements puts them so close to the American column so soon. However Callaghan only knew that the enemy *seemed* to be almost on top of him and that his battle plan was fast unraveling.

Admiral Callaghan barely had time to digest this disturbing information from *Helena* when more disquieting—and more certain—news came in from lead destroyer *Cushing*. She had made visual contact with "three" ships about to cross her bow roughly two-and-a-half miles ahead. (The three were more likely two: the Japanese lead destroyers *Harusame* and *Yudachi*.) These ships had literally come out of nowhere as far as Callaghan was concerned, completely eluding his radar. Suddenly it appeared that two separate groups of enemy ships were on top of his column, one dead ahead and the other to port. He was beset on two sides, and any hope of crossing the T was gone.

On *Cushing*, Commander T. Murray Stokes, division commander of the four van destroyers, now seized the initiative. He requested permission to open fire as he veered *Cushing* to port to bring her torpedoes and guns to bear on the enemy ships ahead. The destroyers behind him moved to follow, and the front of the American line began to crumble.

THE FIRST JAPANESE VESSEL TO SIGHT THE ENEMY WAS *Yudachi*, which reported "unidentified ships ahead" about the time *Cushing* reported visual contact with her. One agonizing minute later, lookouts on *Hiei* reported four enemy cruisers ahead at a range of six miles. Admiral Abe must have wondered why fate was being so unkind to him. His two battleships, armed for a shore bombardment, now faced a surface battle. Was it too late to reload the main battery with armor-piercing shells? The answer came moments later, when *Hiei*'s lookouts sighted what appeared to them as six enemy cruisers and seven destroyers (not far from what was actually there). Abe ordered his formation to turn left so as to bring all his guns to bear. Then he ordered searchlights to illuminate the enemy.

ON THE BRIDGE OF *ATLANTA* THE TENSION HAD become almost unbearable. The TBS frequency was a crackling chaos as the various ships cut in with sighting reports and questions. It was clear the enemy was getting very close, yet still no order to open fire came from the flagship.

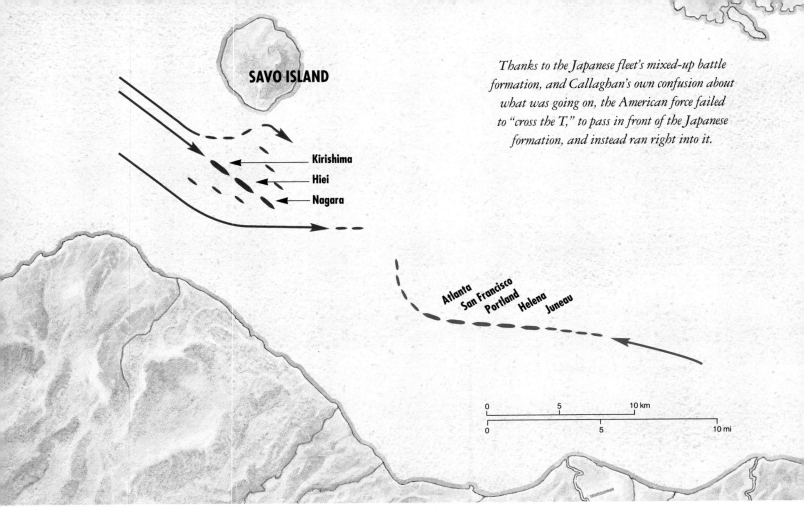

SAVO ISLAND

Kirishima

Hiei

Nagara

Thanks to the Japanese fleet's mixed-up battle formation, and Callaghan's own confusion about what was going on, the American force failed to "cross the T," to pass in front of the Japanese formation, and instead ran right into it.

Atlanta   San Francisco   Portland   Helena   Juneau

0   5   10 km

0   5   10 mi

Finally, in frustration, Admiral Scott growled, "Well, if Admiral Callaghan doesn't say commence firing, I will." Abruptly *Atlanta* confronted a more immediate problem. She had to turn sharply to port to avoid hitting *O'Bannon*, the destroyer immediately in front of her. (As a result of *Cushing's* decision a few minutes earlier to veer to port, the van destroyers following her had become bunched up.) From the bridge of the *San Francisco*, immediately behind *Atlanta*, Admiral Callaghan could see the ship swerve out of line. "What are you doing?" he queried. "Avoiding our destroyers," responded Captain Jenkins. "Come back to your course as soon as you can," the admiral ordered. "You are throwing the whole column into disorder." But any hope of an organized battle formation was already past. When lead destroyer *Cushing* finally followed Callaghan's order and once again turned north, the Japanese cruiser *Nagara* was visible on her starboard bow. This meant the entire American column was steaming into the heart of the enemy formation. The inevitable collision between the approaching forces had happened.

Lieutenant Lloyd Mustin, *Atlanta's* junior gunnery

officer, had listened in growing consternation to the TBS traffic. The admiral's talker had an infuriatingly labored way of slowly enunciating each syllable, when quick crisp orders were surely called for. Merely ordering the two course changes to the north had seemed to take forever. From his position in the after gunnery control he was responsible for the three 5-inch turrets located aft of the rear superstructure. For some minutes now his directors had been tracking two radar targets, speed 20 knots, while the range inexorably closed. As if his words could push the admiral into action, he told the men manning his directors, "This is the real thing. Get ready to shoot!" But still he and all the gunnery officers on thirteen American ships waited.

THROUGH THE 15CM TORPEDO-AIMING TELESCOPE on the *Akatsuki's* bridge, Lieutenant Michiharu Shinya could make out the black silhouettes of several enemy warships on the starboard bow. As he watched, one of them turned toward his ship. It looked like one of the Americans' new single-stack destroyers. "Is it enemy or is it ours?" asked Commander Osamu

Lieutenant Shinya was stationed on Akatsuki's *bridge, clearly visible here. When* Akatsuki's *and* Hiei's *searchlights snapped on, the young torpedo officer saw the cruiser* Atlanta *trapped in their beams.*

Takasuka. "It's an enemy one. No mistake, sir," Shinya quickly replied. But more tantalizing prey were clearly visible. Surely it would be better to let this small ship pass by and attack the bigger game, thought the young torpedo officer. But the captain thought otherwise. "Illuminate with searchlights," he ordered. *Akatsuki*'s searchlight shutters opened almost at the same moment as *Hiei*'s. Both of their powerful beams illuminated a small enemy cruiser.

About this moment—or just before it—Admiral Callaghan finally issued the long-awaited order to fire, but it was not an order to be proud of: "Odd ships fire to starboard, even ships to port." Realizing the mess he had sailed his ships into, he was making the best of a very awkward situation. There were enemy vessels on either side of his fraying column, and there was no other simple way of ensuring that both sets of targets were brought under attack. Almost immediately the plan fell apart. The light cruiser *Atlanta* (number five in line) opened fire to port while the *San Francisco* (number six in line and Callaghan's flagship) opened up to starboard. The battle—or rather the brawl—was on.

Lieutenant Stewart Moredock was standing inside *Atlanta*'s pilothouse when the Japanese searchlight beams hit, casting a long shadow from Captain Jenkins, standing just forward of Moredock. The young lieutenant felt as if the light would burn a hole right through him. Next, with what seemed impossible speed, Moredock watched the ship's forward turrets swing out to port and begin firing. Then the enemy searchlights went out. Any relief, however, was momentary.

In *Atlanta*'s after gunnery control position, Lieutenant Mustin didn't wait for the command to fire. As soon as the enemy searchlights illuminated his ship he simply gave the order: "Action port! Illuminating ship is target. Open fire!" At this point the nearest enemy ship in his sights was less than a mile away, which meant the flight time of his projectiles was little more than two seconds. (Meanwhile *Atlanta*'s forward guns opened fire on *Akatsuki*.)

On *Akatsuki*'s bridge there was an explosion and a blinding flash of light as the whole ship seemed to shake beneath Lieutenant Shinya's feet. Then the concussion blast hit and he was thrown onto the deck. "So now it is my turn to die!" he thought to himself. He felt distant, detached from the material present. Then suddenly he snapped back into awareness. As he struggled to sit up, his head rang as if he had been punched, his right cheek felt hot, and blood trickled down into his right eye.

"Port the helm!" shouted Commander Takasuka, but when Shinya glanced to where the helmsman ordinarily stood, he saw no one. He was close enough to the wheel to try to reach it while still sitting. But when he grasped hold, it swung freely. "She's not answering the helm," he reported. The captain could raise no response from gunnery control and only a handful of the officers on the bridge remained alive. Shinya was reeling from the effects of the blast, having trouble coming to grips with the situation. Then he noticed an unpleasant sticky sensation around his feet. He looked down to discover that his shoes had disappeared—apparently blown off by the blast—and that his socks were slimy with blood.

Akatsuki was out of the battle, according to Shinya, without firing a shot, but one of the two other destroyers in her group, either *Ikazuchi* or *Inazuma*, managed to fire torpedoes at the enemy cruiser. One of these pierced *Atlanta*'s lightly armored side and exploded in the forward engine room, knocking out all but auxiliary diesel power. The torpedo's impact was felt by men in every part of the ship with sickening immediacy. Until now, except for those in a position to actually view the battle, enemy shell hits and *Atlanta*'s own salvoes had been difficult to distinguish. The torpedo was different. In the upper handling room for turret number eight, the aftermost of the ship's 5-inch guns, Seaman Second Class David Driscoll, who had turned eighteen only a few days earlier, heard a distant thud and felt the ship rock. In Battle Two, the secondary conning station located in the after superstructure, Quartermaster First Class George Petyo felt the ship literally lift out of the water as a spray of warm seawater shot over the splinter shield and he was dropped to his haunches by the lurching motion. On the bridge, Quartermaster Third Class Henry Durham was on the communications circuit that linked Battle Two, the engine room, the steering engine room and main damage control when the whole ship shook mightily and he lost communication with the engine room. Moments later the bridge lost steering control, which had to be shifted to the steering engine room. Standing a few steps away from Durham, Stewart Moredock

watched the ship's speed indicator needle sink toward zero as she began to lose way.

The night engagement had quickly degenerated into a chaotic melee as ships nearly rammed each other, fired at constantly shifting targets and changed course and speed in an attempt to gain sailing room. *Hiei*'s course took her toward the four lead American destroyers as they maneuvered frantically to get a fix on her while simultaneously dueling with at least two Japanese destroyers. First *Laffey* charged *Hiei*, barely avoiding a collision as she passed under the battleship's bow, but hitting the bridge with machine-gun fire that killed Captain Masakane Suzuki, Admiral Abe's chief of staff. Although several American destroyers fired torpedoes, none hit home. However, their 5-inch shellfire inflicted some damage to *Hiei*'s superstructure.

Cushing's skipper, Lieutenant Commander Parker, mistakenly believed that at least two of the six torpedoes he fired at a range of about 1,200 yards hit *Hiei*, but he must have been confused by the flashes of her guns or distracted by the terrible beating his own ship was taking. She was caught in a crossfire between the Japanese battleship and other Japanese vessels. Enemy shells soon knocked out her guns, her engines and her steering, killing many of the sailors in exposed positions.

Electrician's Mate First Class William Johnson was safely out of this line of fire. His battle station was with the gyro compass and remote gunnery control in a small room directly below the bridge near the bottom of the ship, but his circumstances were far from comforting. He could hear the pounding of the guns but had no idea how the fight was going. The man beside him, his only companion in the cramped space, had frozen once the battle started. Since his companion wore the only set of headphones, Johnson was cut off from communication with the bridge. He was considering how to bring his shipmate around when the lights went out.

Johnson's first thought was for the gyro compass. If it tumbled it would take hours to get it accurately realigned to north and south. He quickly put the clamps on to hold it in place. Then he grabbed the phones from his fear-paralyzed shipmate and called the bridge. The voice that answered belonged to Bert "Doc" Savage, the ship's cook, whose battle responsibility was bridge talker. "Where are you?" Savage asked. When Johnson told him, he snapped, "Get the hell out of there!" By the light of his battle lantern Johnson managed to push his friend

(Left) William Johnson, stationed deep in the Cushing, was unaware of the battle that her captain, "Butch" Parker (inset), was waging. (Right) Henry Durham of Atlanta.

through the hatch above and out onto the mess deck. As they passed through this open area he noticed two gaping holes in the bulkheads to port and starboard where a shell had passed clear through the ship, barely missing the 37,000-gallon fuel oil tank. When they reached the main deck they found fires raging and dead bodies were everywhere. Johnson left his companion to help a wounded bosun's mate launch the ship's portside whaleboat. But when he cut the fall lines the boat collapsed into the water. Its middle had been blown away.

A T THIS POINT, PERHAPS FIVE MINUTES INTO THE battle, any semblance of organized formation on either side had disappeared as individual Japanese and American commanders acted independently in what had become a series of ship-to-ship encounters. Flames shot from the superstructure of *Hiei*, the Japanese flagship, but she fought on. Undamaged *Kirishima*'s 14-inch guns also lashed out with deadly effectiveness. *Atlanta*, *Cushing* and *Akatsuki* were all in deep trouble— dead in the water and unable to defend themselves. Even someone with a god's-eye view of the situation would have been hard-pressed to guess who was winning—if anyone was.

O N THE BRIDGE OF *AMATSUKAZE*, COMMANDER HARA was momentarily blinded by the flashes of the American shells landing on or near *Hiei*. Seeing that some of these projectiles were passing over the flagship and landing dangerously close to his own vessel, Hara ordered it into action. At top speed *Amatsukaze* charged out from the protection of *Hiei*'s left flank and maneuvered to fire torpedoes. But before Hara could get his bearings, the enemy silhouettes, which he described as "wraith-like images," momentarily disappeared against the dark background of the Guadalcanal coastline. Then three Japanese destroyers passed between him and his targets. When he glanced in the direction of *Hiei*, he saw to his horror that her mast was in flames.

Seeing the three friendly destroyers turn to port, Commander Hara decided to follow in their wake. Suddenly the distinct outlines of several ships in the American column appeared on his starboard bow, the nearest at a range of just over three miles. Perfect. Clearly his torpedo officer thought so, too. "Commander, let's fire the fish!" he shouted. "Get ready, fishermen!" Hara called in reply. Then his ship moved onto an attack course, bearing in on the closest enemy vessel at full speed until the range was less than two miles. "Ready torpedoes. Fire!" the destroyer's skipper ordered. Eight Long Lances dropped into the water and sped toward their target as spray splashed *Amatsukaze*'s bridge. A minute or so later two pillars of fire shot up from the American destroyer (*Barton*). As Hara watched, the ship broke in two and swiftly sank.

Meanwhile *Atlanta* was on fire from hits forward of the bridge, and she was beginning to swing helplessly around to the south. This inadvertently brought her between *San Francisco* and several Japanese ships just as *San Francisco*'s skipper, Captain Cassin Young, was instructing his gunners to switch their fire from a now burning destroyer on his starboard bow to a second destroyer not far behind it. What happened next was every warship commander's nightmare. *San Francisco*'s gunners somehow mistook *Atlanta* for an enemy ship—or failed to see her drift into their line of fire—and sent 8-inch shells crashing into and through her.

Stewart Moredock stood on the starboard side of *Atlanta*'s pilothouse wondering just how badly the torpedo had damaged his ship. He could see fires forward and from somewhere came the hiss of steam. Although he felt no pain, he now realized he'd been wounded during the initial shelling that had sprayed the bridge area with shrapnel. He was bleeding in several places and when he tried to use his right hand, it simply wouldn't function. But he felt neither fear nor anger, only a kind of detachment born of shock. He glanced to the port side of the pilothouse where Captain Jenkins was standing, then looked aft toward the exterior walkway that led from the charthouse to the pilothouse. Admiral Scott had just emerged from the charthouse and was walking forward. Moredock watched him start to take a step, then saw him crumple to the steel decking, dead before he hit the floor. (Three of the admiral's four staff officers died with him.) There was a deafening explosion and the bridge went black.

Two salvoes from *San Francisco*'s main battery slammed into *Atlanta*'s superstructure, setting much of the ship on fire and decimating her command. On the devastated bridge, Stewart Moredock and Captain Jenkins were among the tiny handful to survive. (Jenkins had been moving from port to starboard through the

Atlanta was damaged early on while engaging the enemy. Then, while powerless, the cruiser took several hits on the bridge from 8-inch shells mistakenly fired by the flagship, San Francisco.

pilothouse when the shells hit and somehow escaped with only a wound in the foot.) Moredock was stumbling through the smoke and wreckage trying to figure out what to do next when he bumped into the captain. "Well, we'd better look for a way to get down below and get out of this line of fire," the captain told him. He disappeared in one direction. The young lieutenant went the other.

Moredock limped his way to the starboard rail—one of his legs was now injured—thinking to swing himself over and drop down to the next deck about twenty feet below. Since his right hand was useless, he'd have to depend on his left. But as he pivoted over the side, his left wrist gave a snap, the hand let go and he simply went down, down, landing softly. As he hit, he heard the rush of air being expelled from dead lungs. He had landed on a pile of corpses.

One of the last men left alive on *Atlanta*'s bridge was Quartermaster Third Class Henry Durham. When *San Francisco*'s shells hit, he'd been standing just aft of Chief Quartermaster Rob Roy Latta, who had taken over the wheel at the beginning of the battle. As the lights went out, Latta slumped forward over the wheel, emitting a horrible gurgling sound. Durham dragged his chief to the starboard entry. Then by the light of the fires raging outside, he desperately tried to stanch Latta's chest wound by jamming pieces of shirt into the many holes through which blood bubbled. It was useless. Latta was clearly dead.

Durham then spied a man lying partly in flames on the starboard bridge wing and went to move him. The crossed flags and three chevrons on his sleeve identified him as a signalman first class. He grabbed the man under the shoulders and pulled, but the pull was too easy and the reason gruesomely evident. The man's legs had been cleanly severed at the knees. He, too, was dead. Durham, moving on in search of anyone who was still alive, placed his foot on decking that wasn't there and fell—landing on some very live bodies. This was the crew of the starboard 1.1-inch machine gun tub. The gun captain was extremely irate at Durham's method of arrival. "You could have hurt one of my men," he shouted. The quartermaster scrambled out of the tub and headed aft to see if he could help out at Battle Two.

As the flames spread, *Atlanta* drifted toward the south, away from the action and out of the battle. Of her eight main battery turrets, only numbers seven and

eight remained undamaged. More than two hundred men lay wounded, dying or dead on her decks, and water continued to flow through the torpedo hole in her hull. One of the many casualties was the ship's mascot, Lucky, a black-and-white mongrel, part terrier and part dachshund, who died along with many of the men in repair station number two located in the forward mess hall, below the forward superstructure.

In the stern area of *Atlanta*, at least one officer prematurely ordered abandon ship. This word reached Seaman Second Class David Driscoll and the other men in the upper handling room for 5-inch gun mount number eight, the aftermost twin mount. When Driscoll reached the deck, the order seemed well justified. Forward of his position, the whole superstructure appeared to be burning. He helped take a life raft off the side of one of the after gun mounts, put it over the side and climbed into it with several others. All that he and those with him could think was to get away from the ship before it exploded and sank. (They would all later return to the ship and help try to save her.)

Aboard *San Francisco*, Admiral Callaghan almost certainly realized his gunners' fatal error in firing on *Atlanta*. After the second salvo he ordered "Cease firing own ships." Unfortunately this directive inadvertently went out on the TBS channel, causing confusion and consternation throughout the fractured American column. Few captains obeyed, but many queried the order. Callaghan swiftly clarified: "Give her hell," he ordered. Then, "We want the big ones! Get the big ones first!" His own ship led by example, taking on the enemy flagship at a range of 2,500 yards.

As the cruiser and the battleship traded salvoes, destroyers from both sides joined the fray. But it was *Hiei* that did the most damage, pummeling *San Francisco*'s bridge and secondary control station high in the after superstructure with shells from both her main and secondary batteries. This firestorm killed or wounded all the senior officers. Admiral Callaghan died instantly. Captain Young was mortally wounded. When the exchange of fire was over, Lieutenant Commander Bruce McCandless—the ship's thirty-one-year-old communications officer—found himself in command on the badly damaged bridge. Despite the sad condition of his ship, McCandless turned her west, back into the battle, lest other American ships prematurely follow their retreating flagship. Only after once again engaging the enemy, including trading fire with both *Hiei* and *Kirishima*, did he finally turn his ship east and withdraw out of the line of fire.

In *Cushing*'s wardroom, Lieutenant James Cashman worked furiously to keep up with the flow of wounded men who poured into his first-aid station. Two officers, whose battle stations had been knocked out of action, assisted him and his orderly. These were his roommate, Ensign Eugene Huntemer, and a young lieutenant (junior grade) named Donald Henning. Even with the extra help, the task was overwhelming. Cashman moved among the big oak mess tables that now served as operating tables. The wounded men displayed every imaginable shrapnel injury, from bad cuts to missing arms. In most cases there was little more he could do than apply a tourniquet, dress a wound and administer morphine for pain. Sometimes a limb had to be amputated; occasionally two.

Cashman, with help from Huntemer, was just attempting to put hemostats on a neck wound that had cut a jugular vein when the intercom crackled with the information that Lieutenant Seymour Ruchamkin, the ship's damage control officer, was seriously wounded. "I can't leave my battle station," the doctor curtly replied and continued his work. But Huntemer offered to help fetch the wounded officer. "Well, I'm not ordering you to go," Cashman told his friend, but Huntemer insisted. Just as Huntemer left the wardroom there was a deafening blast and Cashman found himself flat on the floor. The lights had gone out and the room was filled with the acrid smell of explosives. Reflexively he groped for the man with the neck wound to finish applying the hemostats but couldn't find him. (Later he concluded that it was this patient's body combined with the heavy oak table that had acted as a shield and saved his own life.) He never saw Gene Huntemer again.

Electrician's Mate William Johnson, meanwhile, had encountered Lieutenant Commander Parker and Commander Stokes, who had just left the bridge. (It was

Cushing's *medical officer, Lieutenant James Cashman, narrowly avoided death when a shell crashed into the ship's wardroom, where he was tending the wounded.*

the first time Johnson had laid eyes on the ship's new skipper, who had been serving on *Cushing* for just over a month.) Stokes saw that Johnson was carrying a battle lantern and ordered him to blink a recognition signal at a ship that was 500 or 600 yards off to starboard. The answer came in the form of a series of salvoes that plowed into the already dying destroyer (it was likely one of these shells that knocked out the wardroom where Cashman was working). *Cushing* appeared to be doomed, and Lieutenant Commander Parker ordered abandon ship. He sent the division commander off in one of the life rafts, but himself remained on board to oversee the evacuation.

By now the battle had left *Akatsuki* well behind, alone on the darkened water, drifting without engine power, helm, radio or internal communication. On her bridge, Lieutenant Michiharu Shinya stood with the captain and the navigator. No one spoke. There was nothing left to do except wait for the end. Fires enveloped the superstructure aft of the bridge. The destroyer was sinking rapidly. Soon the list to port became so acute that they had to grab onto the window frames of the forward bridge bulkhead in order to remain standing. Finally, with liquid lapping just below the sills, they climbed through the windows and jumped into the tepid water.

Shinya was only a few yards away from the ship when *Akatsuki* settled over onto her port side, pointed her bow up in the air, then gently slipped below the surface. At first the expected suction did not come. Then suddenly he was drawn into an "utterly black abyss." There seemed no point in resisting until a gulp of seawater brought him to his senses. He struggled desperately for the surface, swallowing more water as he fought to escape. When he broke into the air, the surface still swirled roughly from the ship's suction and he gulped as much seawater as oxygen before finally catching his breath. Around him other survivors began calling to each other as they struggled to find anything floating to cling to.

To the west, in the direction of Savo Island, Shinya could see that the battle continued. Despite everything he had been through he could still appreciate the strange beauty of the moment: "The star shells shot up one after the other by the American ships burst so beautifully in the dark sky, and their blue-white light shone brightly on the sea. It was quite an international fireworks display. Now and then shells would whistle past nearby, trailing an unearthly moaning sound behind them."

BY A FEW MINUTES AFTER TWO, WITH THE BATTLE barely fifteen minutes old, each side had drawn considerable blood, but the Americans were in need of a transfusion. *Atlanta* was crippled and burning.

Flagship *San Francisco* had lost communication with the rest of the task force and was now withdrawing. Admirals Scott and Callaghan were both dead. Of the van destroyers only *O'Bannon* had escaped serious injury. *Cushing* was disabled and taking water, *Laffey* was on fire and would sink shortly, and *Sterett* had lost helm control and would soon withdraw. Of the three other cruisers, *Portland* had taken a stern torpedo hit that sliced off her starboard propeller and sculpted her stern plates into an immovable starboard rudder that forced her to steam in a fixed circle. *Atlanta*'s sister ship, *Juneau*, had received a torpedo amidships that possibly broke her keel. She was attempting to limp away from the scene. Only *Helena*, aided by the same superior radar that had enabled her

After Akatsuki *was damaged, the battle left her behind and, with her superstructure on fire, she slowly sank.*

to spot the enemy first, seems to have done more damage than she suffered during the furious opening phase of what had rapidly degenerated, in the words of one American commander, into "a barroom brawl after the lights had been shot out." (She took only superficial hits to the superstructure.) The four destroyers at the rear of the American column had also suffered heavily. *Barton* had sunk and *Monssen* was a flaming wreck.

The Japanese had so far suffered less than the Americans. Although flames shot from the superstructure of Admiral Abe's flagship, *Hiei*, she had not received mortal damage, presumably since none of the American shells were powerful enough to pierce the heaviest armor of her hull. The most damaging hit had jammed *Hiei*'s rudder and opened her aft steering compartment to the sea. Two destroyers were out of the battle—*Akatsuki* had sunk, *Yudachi* was crippled and burning. But the second Japanese battleship, *Kirishima*, had suffered barely a scratch, and light cruiser *Nagara*, although she had been in the thick of the action, had escaped almost as lightly.

The fighting continued for another twenty minutes or so, but the score had not changed much by 0226 when Captain Gilbert Hoover of *Helena*, the senior officer still in radio contact with other American ships, ordered a general withdrawal to the east. Along with *Atlanta*, *Cushing* and *Monssen*, destroyer *Aaron Ward* was unable to obey the call. She had taken nine direct hits, her engine room was flooded, and she was slowly coasting to a stop. Meanwhile most of the Japanese combatants departed to the west, slipping around both sides of Savo Island. The two retreating fleets left behind many sailors on crippled or sinking ships—or already floating in wreckage-strewn water. For them a very long night had just begun.

ELECTRICIAN'S MATE WILLIAM JOHNSON WAS PADDLING a life raft carrying two wounded men away from *Cushing*'s stern when he heard shouts coming from the ship's port side. His two passengers weren't much help—one of them had a hole in his back just to the left of his spine—but he rowed back toward the sound. He found five men gathered just aft of the port torpedo tubes, including Lieutenant Donald Henning, who had been in the wardroom helping Lieutenant Cashman when the lights went out. Henning had suffered only minor wounds when the shell hit, but the men with him were in much worse shape. One fellow had a foot gone; another had lost most of his face. Johnson helped them down a cargo net someone had thoughtfully draped over the side. As Lieutenant Henning came into the raft, he told Johnson, "The captain's still on board." Without really considering the risks, Johnson climbed up the net and went to look for the commanding officer.

He soon found Lieutenant Commander Parker heading aft to check the depth charges. Apparently Parker was concerned that these might detonate as the ship sank, killing men now in the water. Once satisfied that this was not a danger, the two separated to search for survivors. The starboard side of the bridge was on fire, but the ship still floated on an even keel. As Johnson walked forward along the port side, he could see that the port torpedo tubes were trained out as if ready to fire. He went closer until he could make out the figure of a man pinned beneath the outboard tubes. The man was alive, but barely. As hard as he tried, however, there was nothing Johnson could do to free him. So he gave the sailor a cigarette and lit it. Before departing, he left the package and a book of matches within reach, but he doubted whether the poor fellow would have the strength to smoke another.

Johnson's hunt for survivors took him to the machinist's shop, located in the port side of the after deckhouse. When he entered the darkened room he found two men sitting there, quietly, as if the battle had passed them by. Lieutenant David Nickerson, the ship's chief engineer, sat on a rag can with his back resting against the forward bulkhead. In the back corner Machinist's Mate First Class Robert McClung perched on a chair. But neither responded when Johnson spoke and, when he moved closer, the light of his battle lantern revealed that their bellies had been ripped open by shrapnel. Both men were dead.

Johnson and Nickerson had been on *Cushing* together for four years and knew each other well. Johnson was suddenly hit with the thought that the lieutenant had an infant son he would never see. It crossed his mind to remove Nickerson's academy ring and take it to the son as a memento. Then he thought better of the idea. If he died and they found him with Nickerson's ring in his pocket, his superiors would probably think he'd stolen it. (At a *Cushing* reunion in 1984, Johnson told this story to Nickerson's grown-up son Bob, a naval academy graduate like his father and a lieutenant commander in the navy.)

When Johnson and the captain linked up again, he reported that the auxiliary diesel engine was operational and asked if he should try to get some pumps working for fire fighting. "Don't bother," the captain replied. "She's too far gone." And indeed flames had now engulfed most of the forward superstructure and were spreading aft. These made it impossible to reach the man they heard hollering for help from the bow. He identified himself as a seaman named Miller and said his hands were badly burned. In answer to their query, he replied that, yes, he had on a lifejacket. Parker shouted

for him to go over the port side and swim aft. That was the last they heard of him.

As the flames spread farther aft, Parker finally said, "Well, I guess we'd better get the hell out of here." Johnson was wearing a Mae West given him by a pilot *Cushing* had rescued during the Battle of the Santa Cruz Islands in late October. The captain wore only a puny life belt. For extra buoyancy they each tied two empty 5-inch powder cans together with a piece of line, then dropped them into the water. With one can under each arm like waterwings, the captain and the electrician's mate paddled away from the now derelict destroyer.

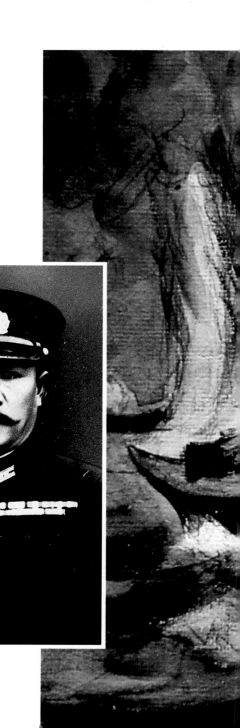

(Right) Yudachi *in battle, as portrayed by one of her crew. She was powerless and badly damaged, but her very gallant captain, Kiyoshi Kikkawa (below), was reluctant to abandon ship.*

YUDACHI'S BATTLE HAD BEEN A WILD ONE. JUST before firing began she had crossed barely in front of *Cushing*, then swung sharply around to port before charging the American column—David against Goliath—firing torpedoes, some of which may have scored on *Portland* and *Juneau*. In the chaos of wheeling ships and blinding shell bursts, she darted in and out, exchanging gunfire with several vessels until she herself was hit—perhaps by friendly fire—and lost engine power. Now with the fighting over, she floated helplessly as her crew fought the fires devouring much of the forward part of the ship. Her men knew that when dawn came they would fall easy prey to the Americans unless

they could somehow get underway. In desperation the executive officer ordered men to bring up hammocks from below to try to rig a makeshift sail to the destroyer's mast. But the idea of trying to sail the ship to the Guadalcanal coast and friendly Japanese troops was a hopeless one.

Around 3 A.M. destroyers *Asagumo* and *Murasame* came alongside *Yudachi* and sized up the situation. Rear Admiral Tamotsu Takama aboard *Asagumo* ordered *Yudachi* abandoned, then he departed, leaving two motorboats to ferry the survivors to Cape Esperance. But Captain Kiyoshi Kikkawa and his crew were reluctant to leave until their ship seemed beyond saving. Thus the

After spending a night floating in the waters of Iron Bottom Sound, Clyde Storey, Leo Spurgeon and Joe Hughes decided to return to the still-smoldering Monssen *when they spotted a shark's dorsal fin near them in the water.*

foot or two of freeboard on the lower side. Occasionally a floatplane, probably from one of the cruisers, flew overhead, but how to attract its attention? Storey went below to grab a bedsheet and started signaling at the next plane that appeared. The ploy worked, the plane landed, and the pilot promised to send out a boat as soon as possible.

The small landing craft, when it finally appeared, kept its distance from the ship, which looked close to capsizing. Eventually the men on board cajoled its coxswain into coming alongside. (Hughes claims Storey brandished a .45 and threatened to shoot; Storey denies he threatened anybody.) All eleven got off the ship. Doughty, who has no recollection of his rescue, woke up in a hospital plane on the way to the American base on Efate. Totally disoriented, the first words he remembers saying were, "Where's my ship?"

It was well into morning before *Cushing* survivor

AT ABOUT 0930, THE MINESWEEPER *BOBOLINK* CAME alongside *Atlanta* and offered her a tow. Once the cable was attached, Henry Durham was detailed to the steering engine room as the final link in a human communication chain. There was no helm control from Battle Two, but there was sufficient auxiliary power to operate the steering gear motor. While engaged in this task, Durham heard shouts indicating that an enemy plane was overhead. "Just my luck," he thought to himself, "to be the lowest man in the ship." The plane turned out to be interested in reconnaissance only and there were no further such incidents. By early afternoon the ship had anchored off Kukum on the western shore of Lunga Point.

One of the first casualties to be ferried ashore was Stewart Moredock. As strong arms lifted him into the waiting Higgins boat, Moredock turned to look at the man on the next stretcher. The man's body was badly wounded, but he was able to lift his head and smile at Moredock—a sweet and innocent smile he never forgot. A few minutes later the man was dead.

Meanwhile the grisly work of collecting the deceased and caring for the wounded continued under the watchful eye of Captain Jenkins, who was often seen walking by with a cane to take pressure off his wounded foot. As the sun grew stronger so did the stench of death. In the after mess hall medical station, the men who'd died during or after surgery were simply piled on the floor. In every part of the ship corpses lay in gruesome poses. Carnage had become commonplace. A young sailor nonchalantly munched on an apple with his free hand while carrying a severed arm to the ship's side to toss it over.

Henry Durham's worst experience during or after the battle came when an officer ordered him to return to the bridge to retrieve the ship's chart. This would prove of enormous use in reconstructing *Atlanta*'s movements for the action report that would have to be filed. The forward ladder was intact and up he went, but he had to climb past the body of a coxswain with whom he'd stood watch on the quarterdeck many a time. When he stepped out of the sun into the wheelhouse, which was still smouldering but no longer on fire, it took a moment for his eyes to adjust. Chief Latta lay where he'd left him, just inside the starboard door. He recognized the body of his division officer, Lieutenant Commander Stewart Smith, the ship's navigator, and of

James Cashman finally caught up with a life raft. Instead of resting, the ship's doctor immediately set to work tending the wounded. He bandaged a sailor's eye that had been blinded by a piece of shrapnel. One man had a loose flap of skin and flesh on his back that exposed his ribcage. Lacking a needle and suturing thread, Cashman closed the wound with safety pins. The able-bodied among the raft's inhabitants rowed them toward Lunga Point, but they seemed to be making little headway. Sometime after noon a Higgins boat came out from Guadalcanal and took everyone on board.

the popular communications officer, Lieutenant Paul Smith, although both were pretty badly torn up.

In the chartroom there was no chart, and no sign of two of his classmates from quartermaster school who had been on duty there when the battle began. Durham got out as quickly as he could. (He saw no sign of Admiral Scott. Later an arm was found with Scott's naval academy ring still on the finger, class of 1911.)

MORE THAN ANYTHING, LIEUTENANT MICHIHARU Shinya wanted to avoid capture, the worst fate the torpedo officer of the sunken *Akatsuki* could imagine. As a Japanese naval officer he had been taught that to be taken prisoner was worse than death. Hard as he tried to swim to land, however, he could make no progress against the current. When an American landing craft passed so near to him that he was tossed in its wake, his heart almost stopped, but the boat did not pause. The sun beat down on his head, making him even more uncomfortable and thirsty. He was coated with oil and saltwater stung his eyes. An open wound gaped on his right hand, and he was suffering from diarrhea, probably caused by all the seawater he had swallowed. Soon it took all his energy just to remain afloat.

Time passed. An enemy floatplane buzzed above him. What was it doing? The awful answer became evident when he heard the sound of nearby boat engines going into reverse. He looked up into the faces of two American sailors reaching over the side of a small landing craft. Summoning two of his few words of English, he spat out, "No thanks." But he lacked the strength to resist the strong arms that pulled him from the water. Inside the boat other Japanese survivors crouched sullenly as he collapsed into a sitting position from which he found it impossible to move. The worst had happened.

BY LATE AFTERNOON CAPTAIN JENKINS CONCLUDED that further efforts to save *Atlanta* were useless. The bulk of the wounded had been transferred ashore, the fires were mostly out, and turrets seven and eight could function, but water continued to come into the ship through the torpedo hole, the list to port was gradually increasing, and ship's engines were beyond repair. Having received Admiral Halsey's permission to make the final decision, Jenkins ordered all but a small demolition party to be taken off the ship. One of the last to leave was Lloyd Mustin. (It wasn't

until that night on Guadalcanal that Mustin realized he'd left his father's naval sword in his cabin.) Although *Atlanta* was not Mustin's first ship, she was very special to him. He was one of her "plank owners," the small corps of officers and enlisted men who had first come on board back in August 1941 when she still sat in the shipyard of the Federal Ship Building and Drydock Company in Kearney, New Jersey. He had sailed on her shakedown voyage and been part of the crew that accepted her into the United States Navy. Mustin got his last look at *Atlanta* at sunset as his boat pulled away from the starboard side, which showed little evidence of battle damage. But the ship's aluminum mast had melted and fallen away to port

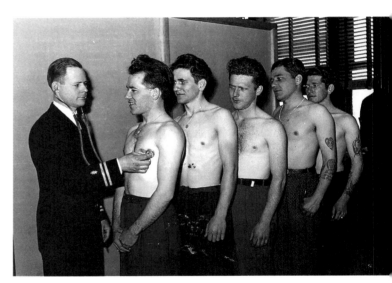

and the forward superstructure was in ruins.

Captain Jenkins directed the demolition crew to set scuttling charges and open all the watertight compartments. Only six men stood at the point of the bow as the captain gave the order and Lieutenant Commander John Wulff, assistant engineering officer, pushed down the plunger on the detonator. The deck shook slightly, a muffled explosion came from astern, then the men climbed down a cargo net into the waiting launch. Captain Jenkins was the last. He insisted the boat remain close by until the ship was gone—about 8 P.M.

So ended the first and by far the bloodier part of what has come to be known as the Naval Battle of Guadalcanal. The first round had clearly gone to the Japanese, at least in terms of ships lost or damaged and men killed or wounded. (In addition to the American ship toll from the night action, wounded *Juneau* was torpedoed at noon by a Japanese submarine as what remained of Admiral Callaghan's task force retreated to the south. She sank immediately and her surviving crew were left to their fate.) But Admiral Abe's striking force had been thwarted in its main purpose—to bombard the airfield out of action. And the large reinforcement convoy under the command of the maestro of the Tokyo Express, Admiral Tanaka, turned back to the naval base in the Shortland Islands. But the Japanese did not give up their plan. The most decisive naval contest of the entire Guadalcanal campaign was far from over.

When Juneau *(bottom) was sunk by a torpedo on November 13, five brothers were among her crew. The subject of publicity when they enlisted (far left), the five Sullivans (left, from left to right), Joseph, Francis, Albert, Madison and George, overcame official reluctance and served together on the same ship. Four went down with the* Juneau, *and the fifth, George, died in a life raft awaiting rescue. The Sullivans became national heroes (below), the subject of a Hollywood movie,* The Fighting Sullivans, *and had a destroyer, U.S.S.* The Sullivans, *named for them.*

the five Sullivan brothers
"missing in action" off the Solomons

THEY DID THEIR PART

147

GRAVEYARD OF THE DESTROYERS

LIKE FALLEN FOOTSOLDIERS, THE DESTROYERS
LOST ON THE FIRST NIGHT OF THE NAVAL
BATTLE OF GUADALCANAL LIE IN SILENCE ON
THE SUBMERGED BATTLEFIELD.

Inside Sea Cliff's *cramped control cabin.*

IN THE COURSE OF OUR 1992 EXPEDITION WE
found four of the six destroyers that sank during or shortly after the first phase of the Naval
Battle of Guadalcanal. (A fifth, *Cushing*, had been
located the year before.) These four wrecks—one
Japanese and three American—form a haunting
pictorial record of that battle's brutal frenzy. These
small unarmored ships were no match for the
cruiser and battleship batteries they faced. They
depended on speed, maneuverability and the effectiveness of their torpedoes. But the American Mark
XV torpedo was vastly inferior to the Japanese
Long Lance, which packed more explosive power,

was faster, had a range over three times longer and—most important of all—usually exploded on impact. During this night brawl there is no evidence that a single American torpedo detonated on a target, whereas the Japanese variety accounted for known hits on *Atlanta*, *Portland*, *Juneau*, *Barton*, and *Laffey*.

The destroyers were the naval foot soldiers in the battle, and as often happens to loyal foot soldiers, they suffered more than the elite troops. The wrecks we filmed,

each one posed differently in death, made me think of Matthew Brady's haunting photographs of Civil War dead. They also reminded me of that chilling picture of the slain Japanese soldiers lying on the sandbar across the mouth of Alligator Creek the day after Colonel Ichiki's rash attack against a superior American force.

I'll never forget our first look at *Barton*, which was split in two by torpedoes from *Yudachi*. We found only the bow section, lying on its side.

Yudachi didn't suffer quite as much, but she was fairly badly torn up from an explosion in her after magazine that left the stern portion of the ship in ruins. The forward tip of her bow had fallen off—probably on impact—and was lying on the bottom. Her bridge, although it had collapsed somewhat to port, was still recognizable, with speaking tubes visible. *Monssen*, which burned for many hours before sinking, was upright and in one piece, although her bridge had vanished. *Laffey*, had lost her stern third, but the whole bridge, the torpedo tubes and both forward 5-inch guns were all still in place.

These images are grim evidence of the confusion and horror of the chaotic night battle of November 13, which contributed so many ships to the graveyard of Iron Bottom Sound.

MONSSEN

HIT BY NO FEWER THAN THIRTY-THREE SHELLS, THREE OF BATTLESHIP CALIBER, THE U.S.S. *MONSSEN* CAUGHT FIRE AND BURNED THROUGHOUT THE NIGHT OF NOVEMBER 13, 1942.

(Above) Amidships on Monssen, *the deck plating around her torpedo tubes has been badly damaged by corrosion. (Top) The destroyer's number two gun* mount, just forward of the bridge, has lost its cover. (Right) Working in tandem, Scorpio *and* Sea Cliff *investigate* Monssen.

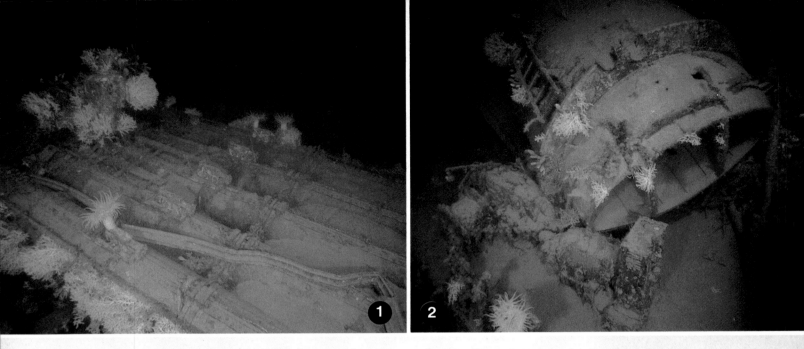

(Below) Monssen *as she appeared before the war. Prior to the* Guadalcanal *campaign, the gun just to the rear of her second stack was removed as was the small deckhouse. Otherwise, she looks largely as she did when sunk.*

1. *One of her quintuple banks of torpedo tubes.*
2. *Her forward stack is now down and lying on deck on its side.*

3. *A view of her number two gun, showing that it has jumped its cradle.*

4. *The "bull nose" ring at the very tip of her bow, though encrusted with marine growth, is still easy to identify.*

BARTON

HIT BY JAPANESE TORPEDOES AT THE HEIGHT
OF THE FIGHTING ON THE FIRST NIGHT OF
THE NAVAL BATTLE OF GUADALCANAL,
THIS DESTROYER BROKE APART AND QUICKLY SANK,
TAKING MOST OF HER CREW WITH HER.

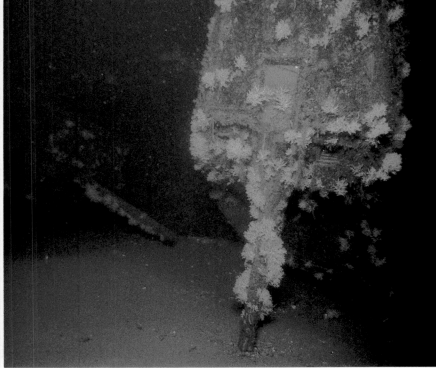

(Left) The Barton's bow
looms out of the darkness.
This forward portion of the
ship extends back about one
hundred feet, ending

abruptly just before the
bridge. (Above) The
Barton's two forward
5-inch guns now thrust
downward into the mud.

LAFFEY

JUMPED BY THREE JAPANESE DESTROYERS AFTER SHE SPRAYED
THE JAPANESE BATTLESHIP *HIEI* WITH MACHINE-GUN FIRE DURING THE
NAVAL BATTLE OF GUADALCANAL, *LAFFEY* LOST HER STERN TO A LONG LANCE
TORPEDO, EXPLODED, AND SWIFTLY SANK.

Laffey's wounds, although fatal, left her forward part in remarkably good condition. (Top left) Her bridge wings are skeletal but still present, and the round ports of her charthouse are recognizable. (Top right) Her bow seems to be cutting through the mud of Iron Bottom Sound. (Above left) Laffey's torpedo tubes and deckhouse (above) and one of the boat davits (right) shown below are still visible.

YUDACHI

After a night of wild battle on November 13, 1942, the damaged *Yudachi* was left drifting helplessly. Finally she was sent to the bottom by shells from the U.S.S. *Portland* that blew up her aft magazine.

Teiji Nakamura (above), a junior officer on Yudachi *(top), survived the sinking. Here he poses beside* Yudachi's *forward gun mount. (Right)* Sea Cliff *closes in on* Yudachi. *Her bow, which is lying on its side, was probably sheared off on impact with the bottom. On her bridge, now completely exposed, are the voice tubes that were used for communicating orders throughout the ship.*

(Top) One of Yudachi's *batteries of 24-inch Long Lance torpedoes. (Above) Another view of* Yudachi's *bridge. Its sharp angle (right) is probably due to corrosion that has collapsed shell-damaged plating, tipping the entire bridge over to the port side. The degaussing cable visible on the ship's side (and in the picture below) identifies the wreck as Japanese. Allied vessels didn't usually carry this device for demagnetizing the hull externally. The railing support matches that in the picture (inset) of Teiji Nakamura with his friend Lieutenant Kabashima, who painted the view of* Yudachi *seen on pages 140-141.*

CHAPTER SIX

NIGHT OF THE BIG GUNS

November 14-15, 1942

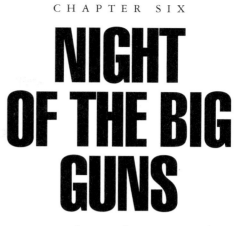

CAPTAIN THOMAS L. GATCH OF U.S.S. *South Dakota* had not been sleeping well. The nasty wound he'd suffered during the Battle of the Santa Cruz Islands still bothered him. His left arm was temporarily paralyzed and in a sling.

The injury had happened as his battleship's powerful anti-aircraft batteries mowed down the Japanese planes that were attempting to knock out aircraft carrier *Enterprise*.

(Left) With Savo Island visible over her stern, the U.S.S. Washington *fires at the Japanese. (Above)* South Dakota's *commanding officer, Thomas L. Gatch.*

One Kate managed to drop a 500-pound bomb that landed atop turret number one, splattering against the turret's heavy armor like a bug against a windshield and sending shrapnel flying toward the bridge. One fragment sliced Gatch's jugular vein and only quick action by those beside him prevented him from bleeding to death.

Still, with fresh battles in the offing, he had insisted on resuming his command, and Rear Admiral Willis Augustus Lee had agreed.

While the awful events of the early hours of November 13 played themselves out in Iron Bottom Sound, *South Dakota*, along with the battleship *Washington*, maneuvered as part of a powerful escort for the aircraft carrier *Enterprise* about 400 miles to the south of Guadalcanal. But when Admiral Halsey learned of the deaths of Admirals Scott and Callaghan and the steep costs of their battle, he realized he had almost nothing left to counter the next Japanese move—except his two big battlewagons. Some of his staff counseled against risking these precious naval assets in the restricted waters around Guadalcanal, but to Halsey the choice was simple. Either he sent in these ships or he left Henderson Field to the mercy of the Japanese navy. It was a gamble he felt he had to take.

On the afternoon of November 13, while both *Hiei* and *Atlanta* were entering their final death throes, Admiral Lee on *Washington* received Halsey's orders to proceed with four escorting destroyers directly to Guadalcanal. It was too late for this force to reach the island that night and, as his six ships turned their prows northward, he knew that during the coming darkness the field was wide open for the enemy. Not surprisingly, the Japanese were prepared to seize the opportunity.

As darkness fell, Vice Admiral Gunichi Mikawa, victor of Savo Island and still commander of the Eighth Fleet based at Rabaul, led a strong bombardment force of heavy and light cruisers down the Slot toward Guadalcanal. Their job was to accomplish the task at which Admiral Abe had failed: eliminate Henderson Field as a threat to Admiral Tanaka's troop convoy that was now rescheduled for the night of November 14-15. Mikawa's ships fired almost one thousand 8-inch shells at the airfield, but despite help from flares dropped by spotting planes, they missed the main airstrip and damaged only a few aircraft. Nonetheless the fires visible after the bombardment convinced the admiral that he had delivered a heavy blow. So, as he withdrew, Admiral Tanaka's convoy once again left the Shortland Islands and began steaming down the Slot. His landings were to be covered by yet another bombardment group, this time led by *Kirishima* (the surviving battleship from the November 13 battle) and under the command of Vice Admiral Nobutake Kondo.

Mikawa quickly discovered just how ineffectual his bombardment had been. With daylight on the fourteenth, successive waves of Guadalcanal-based airplanes and flights from the carrier *Enterprise* (now within striking range of Guadalacanal) mauled first his

(Above) *Willis Lee commanded the task force made up of* Washington, South Dakota *and four destroyers.* (Below) South Dakota *under attack at the Battle of the Santa Cruz Islands, where she had suffered a bomb hit on her number one turret that nearly killed Captain Gatch.*

own task force, then Tanaka's convoy. By mid-afternoon Tanaka had lost six transports and a seventh was on its way back to the Shortlands along with two destroyers bearing more than 1,500 survivors. Only four of the original eleven transports remained; and four of his remaining ten destroyers were so crowded with soldiers rescued from the disabled ships that they would have been useless in a fight. Worse, the attacks had so slowed his progress that, given his transports' top speed of 13 knots, he could not possibly reach the landing point until nearly dawn on November 15, which would expose him to more air attacks. Even the man Samuel Eliot Morison referred to as "tenacious Tanaka" doubted the wisdom of continuing. But when he learned that Admiral Kondo was speeding southward to bombard Henderson Field and provide him with surface support, he obeyed the order to proceed "with a feeling of relief."

Admiral Lee had greeted Halsey's order to head for Guadalcanal with gusto. Finally he and his two power-ful battleships would have a chance to meet the Japanese head to head and prove what they could do. No matter that neither *Washington* nor *South Dakota* had ever engaged another surface ship in battle. Their 16-inch gun crews had drilled to the point of numbness and become so proficient that they could reload their giant 1.35-ton projectiles in less than fifteen seconds, even though the manual said it took thirty. No matter that Lee's four destroyers had never before operated together and that two of them lacked even gun control radar, a severe handicap in night fighting. He and his men were aching for action.

Willis Lee was himself new to the South Pacific the-ater, but he seems to have been well suited to the task at hand. Before *Washington*, he had flown his flag briefly from *South Dakota* (until an uncharted reef at Tongatapu sent her back to Pearl Harbor for repairs). He was known to both crews as a down-to-earth admiral who always had a cheerful greeting for officer and enlisted man alike. He smoked an endless chain of Philip Morris cigarettes and liked to relax with a paperback Western, but above all he liked to talk gunnery. When he joined *Washington* he had instituted the Gun Club, a group of senior officers who met almost daily to discuss ballistic problems. He knew everything his ships' nine 16-inch guns and powerful arrays of twin-mounted 5-inchers could do. Even more important, perhaps, he was a student of radar. His two battleships possessed not only

The heart of the battleships' power was their big guns. (Above) Using a portable crane, members of South Dakota's crew help load the ship with 16-inch shells to be stored (below left) in the ship's armor-plated shell rooms. (Below, right) A sailor works inside one of South Dakota's 16-inch guns. (Right) A 16-inch gun being readied for firing aboard a battleship.

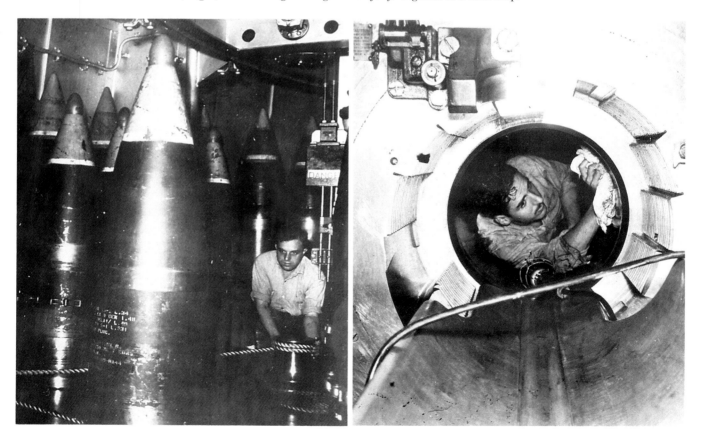

the best—the new SG type—but he knew how to use it, in vivid contrast to the late admirals Scott and Callaghan.

Lee realized he would likely be facing a numerically superior enemy force that would almost certainly include battleships, although he knew that one-on-one the First-World-War-vintage *Kongo* class ships were no match for his state-of-the-art gun platforms. His 16-inch shells could pierce the thickest enemy armor even at maximum range while the Japanese 14-inch projectiles could penetrate his 12-inch-thick armor belts only at relatively close quarters. But close quarters was what awaited him in Iron Bottom Sound. In those narrow waters, where long-distance gun battles were unlikely, the sheer size of his battleships added all sorts of risks, particularly against an enemy whose superiority with torpedoes in night actions was already well proven.

Undaunted, Lee formed a daring battle plan. Just after dusk on the night of the fourteenth, he would briefly scour the waters west of Guadalcanal to search for the Japanese reinforcement convoy, then wheel north of Savo Island and into Iron Bottom Sound, sweeping southeast past Lunga Point, then west along the Guadalcanal coast and exiting to the south of Savo. His aim was to surprise and annihilate any enemy force he encountered, and prevent any reinforcement convoy from unloading.

By late afternoon on November 14, Vice Admiral Nobutake Kondo knew that his bombardment mission would likely meet some opposition, but most aerial reconnaissance reports had grossly underestimated the strength of the force that was steaming to meet him, causing him to conclude that the largest ships he would be facing were heavy cruisers. Kondo's force of one battleship, four cruisers and nine destroyers would be more than a match for these.

But was Kondo a match for Admiral Lee? He had not, it seems, marked himself as a particularly wily or aggressive commander. In the opinion of many of his contemporaries he

Vice-Admiral Nobutake Kondo was ordered to carry out the Henderson Field bombardment that had been thwarted by the first night action of the Naval Battle of Guadalcanal.

lacked combativeness and had failed to seize opportunities during the two great carrier battles fought east of Guadalcanal in the previous months. Commander Tameichi Hara, who commanded destroyer *Amatsukaze* during the November 13 battle, was not among Kondo's fans, dismissing him as an "amiable and affable" scholar and a "British gentleman sort of man" who lacked fighting spirit. "It is still a mystery to me why Yamamoto thought so highly of Kondo," Hara later commented, "even after his half-hearted actions in two earlier important battles." It seemed that Yamamoto had replaced Admiral Abe with another cautious commander.

Just after 4 P.M. *Washington*'s popular captain, Glenn Davis, addressed his men over the ship's loudspeaker system. "We are going into an action area. We have no great certainty what forces we will encounter. We might be ambushed. A disaster of some sort may come upon us. But whatever it is we are going into, I hope to bring all of you back alive. Good luck to all of us." This less than stirring speech does not seem to have dampened the already high morale on Admiral Lee's flagship. On *South Dakota*, Captain Gatch gave a more upbeat pep talk. (According to Ralph Ingram, Jr., author of an as yet unpublished book about *South Dakota*, Gatch displayed an engaging common touch. Not a stickler for navy protocol, he demonstrated "great compassion for his men" and made a point of regularly visiting every part of his vast ship.) Gatch's brief oration closed with the words, "Are you ready?" to which his crew chorused in reply, "Yeah! Let's go get them."

As darkness fell and Cape Esperance drew near on their starboard bows, the American task force went to general quarters and Lee followed a course west of Guadalcanal to a position 21 miles northwest of Savo Island. Thanks to a light breeze from the east, sailors in exposed positions could catch the sweet smell of tropical flowers. Commander Raymond Hunter, *Washington*'s officer of the deck, later described

(Above) Before being sent to the Solomons, Washington *had served in the Atlantic until well into 1942. Here she is shown at Hvalfjord, Iceland. (Inset) A drawing of her popular skipper, Glenn Davis, by Dwight Shepler.*

it as a "heavenly aroma." It made other sailors think of gardenias and honeysuckle, but for many the cloying odor soon became associated with the sickly smell of death.

At 2110 Lee formed his ships into a line—the four destroyers leading, followed by *Washington* and *South Dakota*—and proceeded east, then southeast, on a course that would take them north of Savo and into Iron Bottom Sound at a moderate speed of 17 knots. The sea was calm and a pale quarter moon was rising into a sky filmed with a thin, high overcast. Scattered squalls grumbled on the horizon and low cirrus clouds hung over the sound. The men at their stations in the two great battlewagons and the four puny-seeming destroyers sat tense and expectant. In *South Dakota*'s number one turret (nicknamed "the bomb shelter" after it survived the direct hit that injured Captain Gatch during Santa Cruz), the

turret commander, Ensign Gerald Norton, and his men awaited the long-anticipated order to fire their first 16-inch salvo in a real battle. In "officer's country," a damage control crew numbering fifty to sixty men filled the passageway running across the front of the main deck superstructure and spilled aft into the officers' wardroom. Gunner's Mate Third Class Charles Carpenter lounged in a barber's chair that had been incongruously placed at the starboard end of the passage, considering himself lucky to have found such a comfortable seat. In the radio transmitting room below the armored deck, Warrant Radio Electrician Kenneth Jenkins waited and sweated. The ventilators were shut when the ship closed down for battle, and it got so close that one man was detailed simply to mop up the perspiration. His crew's job was to monitor the frequencies of enemy radio transmissions. None of them understood Japanese, but each

(Top) Kondo's flagship was the heavy cruiser Atago, *a veteran of many battles in the South Pacific and a fixture in the prewar Japanese navy, when such activites as (above left) sumo wrestling on the stern and (above right) a judo class took place. (Below) The destroyer* Ayanami. *On the night of November 14-15, she found herself facing the entire American fleet alone.*

burst of gibberish was louder than the one before. The enemy was getting closer.

As Admiral Lee's task force began filing into the sound, three PT boats from Tulagi spotted him. One of the PT skippers was picked up by *Washington*'s radio as he commented, "There go two big ones, but I don't know whose they are!" Lee, who didn't know the current local code, immediately called Radio Guadalcanal with the following message: "Refer your big boss about Ching Lee; Chinese, catchee? Call off your boys." The "big boss" was Lee's old friend Archer Vandegrift, "Ching" Lee's nickname from his Annapolis days. This bit of extemporizing worked perfectly: Lee was a well-known figure. The PT boat skipper overheard Lee's message for the marine commander and immediately cut in, "Identity established. We are not after you."

Lee had also been spotted by Kondo's advance guard under Rear Admiral Shintaro Hashimoto, coming down from the north with a light cruiser and three destroyers to sweep the area for any sign of the enemy. As he approached, Hashimoto's lookouts glimpsed the dark shapes of enemy ships north of Savo, but reinforced the error of earlier reconnaissance reports by identifying the big silhouettes as cruisers—nothing for Kondo to worry about. Hashimoto detached one destroyer, *Ayanami*, to sweep around Savo in a counterclockwise direction and make sure that coast was clear for the arrival of his boss's bombardment unit. Meanwhile he would pursue the just-sighted enemy force with his flagship *Sendai* and his two remaining destroyers.

With this act, Admiral Kondo's considerable forces became split in four. Kondo had earlier detached Admiral Susumu Kimura aboard light cruiser *Nagara* with four destroyers to screen well ahead of his bombardment group, which would linger at the rear until he knew the coast was clear. Thus his bombardment force of heavy cruisers *Atago* (his flagship) and *Takao*, with battleship *Kirishima* and two destroyers, was unavailable as the battle was about to be joined.

At 2252 Admiral Lee's lead destroyer, *Walke*, reached a position north of Lunga Point and made the planned starboard turn to head due west. Then one by one the five remaining ships in the American line followed. As soon as Lee's flagship made the turn, his SG radar—blind in a broad arc astern because it had been mounted on the front of the tower foremast, not on the top—made contact with Admiral Hashimoto's three ships entering the sound northeast of Savo. The time was 2300. High in the tower masts on both battleships, the gunnery control officers quickly got the enemy in their sights. At 2316 Admiral Lee ordered, "Open fire when you are ready." The range was just over 10 1/2 miles. A minute later all nine of *Washington*'s 16-inchers let forth with a mighty roar. Within another minute, *South Dakota* followed suit. "Our ship gave a convulsive, sidewise whip, as all three turrets let go at once," Captain Gatch later wrote. Finally these two behemoths were doing what they were supposed to.

To Gatch and others on *South Dakota*'s bridge, it appeared that two of the three enemy ships were hit and that at least one was on fire. But this was a typically overoptimistic battle illusion, here enhanced by Hashimoto's quick reaction to being straddled by enemy shells. The Japanese commander made smoke and temporarily withdrew to the north. The first phase of the battle was thus quickly over without either side drawing blood.

Now the four American destroyers, with *Walke* in the lead, opened the second phase of the contest. Approaching a point south of Savo just as lone *Ayanami* was rounding the bend of the island from the other direction, *Walke*'s gun control radar picked up the Japanese destroyer and opened fire. Moments later the other three American destroyers joined in. Then the Americans spotted Kimura's screening force, the cruiser *Nagara* and four destroyers coming in from the north, and brought them under fire. But the Japanese fired back furiously while they maneuvered to launch their deadly Long Lance torpedoes.

The first ship to suffer on either side was *Preston*, number three in the American line, probably from *Nagara*'s 5 1/2-inch main battery. Within minutes the American destroyer was aflame and sinking, the majority of her crew dead, the survivors hastily abandoning ship. In short order *Walke*'s bow was blown off and she too was abandoned and sank. The remaining two destroyers, *Gwin* and *Benham*, were seriously damaged and soon ordered to withdraw. But *Ayanami* paid a price for being the closest and most visible Japanese ship. *South Dakota*'s and *Washington*'s 5-inch guns soon put the Japanese destroyer out of commission. Meanwhile Kimura's screening force withdrew to the west, leaving *Ayanami* behind, drifting powerless and on fire.

And so, although the main units of the contending

forces had not yet engaged, Admiral Lee had completely lost his destroyer screen. But this sacrifice surely saved him from taking any torpedo hits. (The destroyers "probably saved our bacon," Lee later wrote.) He was down to his two battleships and about to prove whether Halsey's gamble had been worth taking.

At 2330, as *Washington* and *South Dakota* bore down on their crippled destroyer van, *South Dakota*'s radio, radar screens and fire control equipment suddenly went dead. It was "like being blindfolded," Gatch later wrote. A short circuit in one of the engine

room switchboards had knocked out much of her electrical power. As the electricians scrambled to diagnose and treat the problem, her guns went silent. Captain Gatch had lost touch with a complex tactical situation at a critical moment. The battle was barely twenty minutes old.

On *Washington*'s bridge Commander Hunter didn't have time to worry about the sudden loss of communication with *South Dakota*. As officer of the deck he was responsible for keeping his ship out of trouble, and trouble was dead ahead. Directly in *Washington*'s path lay the burning and sinking American destroyers. The water was littered with sailors who had already abandoned ship. At a speed of 26 knots, there really wasn't much time to consider the options. All Hunter remembers now is that he ordered the helmsman, "Come left. Come left." His aim was to keep the blazing destroyers between his ship and the enemy. The helmsman did as instructed, and the great ship narrowly sidestepped the obstacle before resuming her westward course. *Washington*'s executive officer, Commander Arthur Ayrault, saw what was happening and rushed aft from Battle Two to the closest damage control station. He ordered its crew to turn out on deck and cut loose the life rafts tethered on the starboard side—quick thinking that undoubtedly saved many lives.

South Dakota's lost radar vision returned just as she was turning left to follow *Washington*'s sidestep (the power loss had lasted about three minutes). Suddenly Captain Gatch ordered a sharp course change to starboard, one that would leave the damaged destroyers to port. The reason Gatch changed his mind remains obscure—perhaps his initial left turn brought him on a collision course with one of his own destroyers—but the result was doubly damaging. When he resumed a westward course, *South Dakota* was steaming between the burning American ships and the advancing Japanese, thus presenting a nicely backlit silhouette for their gunners. What's more, he'd managed to position himself in *Washington*'s radar-blind starboard quarter. In one stroke Captain Gatch had inadvertently placed his ship where the enemy could see it but Admiral Lee couldn't.

Washington, with *South Dakota* now about a mile astern and off her starboard quarter, sailed southwest of Savo toward more open water just as Admiral Hashimoto returned to the fray. Hashimoto's three ships—*Sendai* and the two destroyers that had cagily dodged American salvoes at the battle's opening—had turned around and were again storming in from the north, down the east

side of Savo Island. (Admiral Kimura's screening group had withdrawn toward Admiral Kondo's bombardment group, which marked time northwest of Savo, waiting for the tactical situation to become more clear.) At 2340 *South Dakota* began firing on Hashimoto's ships, which had been sighted astern. But the only damage was self-inflicted. *South Dakota*'s rear turret set fire to the three floatplanes perched on her quarterdeck, further increasing her visibility. Fortunately the next salvo blasted two of the planes overboard and blew out the fire on the one that remained. At this supremely inopportune moment another electrical problem knocked out *South Dakota*'s SG radar.

Admiral Kondo, aboard the heavy cruiser *Atago*, still refused to believe he faced enemy capital ships. He was more concerned about reports of a possible second enemy force advancing from the west (Tanaka's convoy,

(Left) South Dakota's *forward turrets fire a salvo. (Above) On* South Dakota's *after deck the morning following the battle, the one remaining scout plane shows the damage it had received from the big guns that also blasted the two other planes overboard.*

as it turned out) than the enemy fleet his forward ships had already engaged and, based on a report from *Ayanami*, defeated. So confident was he that this puny American force was on the run, that he decided to proceed with his bombardment mission and laid in a course for Lunga Point, ordering Admiral Hashimoto to sweep east ahead of him. Hashimoto obeyed, leaving destroyer *Uranami* to tend to the injured *Ayanami*, still drifting

(Overleaf) The Japanese battleship Kirishima *(left) takes hit after hit from* Washington *as the battle reaches its climax.*

southeast of Savo. This took cruiser *Sendai* and destroyer *Shikanami* out of the battle just as Kondo was about to want their help. The commanding Japanese admiral was now on a roughly converging course with the two American battleships emerging from the sound south of Savo and about to receive the surprise of his life.

Moments before midnight *South Dakota*'s balky radar came back on, just in time to pick up Kondo's force off her starboard bow at a range of a little over three miles. But before her gunners could get a fix on the Japanese, enemy searchlights exposed the American battleship's unmistakable outline to the astonished Admiral Kondo, who ordered every gun and torpedo fired her way. None of the Long Lances hit, but Japanese shells tore through *South Dakota*'s tower foremast, killing many of the gunnery control personnel, wiping out the entire crew in the radar plotting room and knocking out gun directors and radars. (*Washington* would have joined this battle sooner, but Lee was still unsure of *South Dakota*'s position and feared firing on his other battleship.) Captain Gatch fought back, but it seems that none of his shells found enemy targets.

By the time the first Japanese salvoes pierced *South Dakota*'s superstructure, Charles Carpenter had vacated his barber's chair for a safer spot at the portside end of the passage, away from the direction of Japanese fire. But a friend who had been egging him to give up this privileged perch immediately took Carpenter's place. Soon after, one of those enemy shells passed through the starboard end of the passage, taking his friend in the barber's chair and quite a few others with it.

Suddenly it seemed safer to be out on deck, so Carpenter and several others sought shelter behind turret two. The noise wasn't too bad until curiosity overcame him and he stuck his head around the barbette just as the turret's three guns erupted. The blast knocked Carpenter off his feet and left him temporarily deaf.

As in all such naval battles, there were many stories of hairsbreadth escapes, but the most remarkable on *South Dakota* was surely that of Commander I. W. Gorton, the ship's supply officer. During the battle he was stationed on a catwalk outside secondary control, atop the after superstructure, from where he broadcast a play-by-play of the action over the ship's loudspeaker system. Once the ship came under heavy fire, he was forced to retreat inside the superstructure, only to be driven outside again by hot steam from a ruptured line

(someone had forgotten to turn off the ship's whistle before the battle). Battle Two, about twenty feet aft, seemed a safer destination, but he'd taken only a few steps in its direction when a shell crashed through the armor overhead, its concussion smashing him headfirst against a bulkhead. Only his steel helmet saved him from serious injury. He was struggling to his feet when another shell missed him by inches, blasting him onto his back. Miraculously Gorton was still unwounded. He crawled to within a few feet of Battle Two, then leapt the rest of the way.

But the ship's secondary conning position was more hell than haven. Another ruptured line jetted scalding steam into the enclosure, and a fire on the deck below heated the floor to the point that a quartermaster who'd lost a shoe was hopping around on the other foot. The ship's executive officer, Commander Archibald Uehlinger, was faced with a difficult decision: abandon this crucial post or tough it out. The uninjured crewmen gathered in Battle Two were beginning to panic. One of them started muttering, "My God, how scared I am!" but when Uehlinger snapped, "Shut up. I'll do the talking here," the panic subsided. Surrounded by choking steam mixed with smoke, the exec decided to hang on. Soon the steam line was shut off and the fire below brought under control. But it was a near thing.

As the enemy fusillade continued, Captain Gatch ordered speed increased to 27 knots and bravely fought on. To Admiral Lee's query, "Are you all right?" Gatch replied almost nonchalantly, "Everything seems okay." That was his last communication during the battle. *South Dakota*'s radio antennae were soon shot away as enemy fire continued to punish her upper works. In roughly four minutes, the battleship suffered twenty-seven hits, including at least one 14-incher. Her heavy armor held and she could still fire most of her guns, but she could not properly aim them. To quote Admiral Lee, she was "deaf, dumb, blind and impotent."

While *South Dakota* took the heat, *Washington* took aim, dividing up the enemy targets between her 5-inch and 16-inch guns—the latter honing in on *Kirishima*. (First her destroyers, then *South Dakota* had served as decoys, and so far Lee's flagship had gone undetected by Kondo.) Cruisers *Atago* and *Takao* eluded most of the enemy fire, but *Kirishima* took a pounding. Shells perforated her hull below the water line, jammed her rudders to port and knocked out two of her four 14-inch turrets. At nine minutes after midnight, Admiral Kondo pulled back his cruisers, apparently worried about protecting Tanaka's approaching convoy. This left *Kirishima* sailing in long helpless loops as her crew struggled to regain helm control. Once Kondo sighted the convoy, still well to the west, he turned back toward the enemy. To his amazement he now sighted a second enemy battleship, farther away. But the closer battlewagon (*South Dakota*) was his primary concern. He fired torpedoes then saw her turn away to the south.

None of these torpedoes hit *South Dakota*, but Captain Gatch's ship had already suffered grievous wounds, though not mortal ones. He recognized his powerful battlewagon was now more a liability than an asset and, at 0010, he elected to withdraw. This prudent act left *Washington* alone to face the entire Japanese force. But the battle was for all practical purposes over. For the next twenty minutes or so, Lee played cat and mouse with an enemy that unsuccessfully tried to skewer him with Long Lances. Finally he decided his best course was also to withdraw. (Pursuing Japanese destroyers launched several more spreads of torpedoes, some coming uncomfortably close, but none hitting.) He would leave the approaching Japanese convoy to the airmen of the Cactus Air Force.

Admiral Kondo was also in the process of choosing discretion over his other options. About the time Lee decided to withdraw, Admiral Kondo canceled the bombardment mission and retired, not wishing to expose his remaining warships to a daylight air attack. He had done well against a powerful foe, later claiming that he had sunk at least one and possibly two battleships, two cruisers and two destroyers. The way was now clear for the convoy to advance.

He left behind not only disabled *Kirishima* but powerless *Ayanami*. The burning destroyer lasted until 0200.

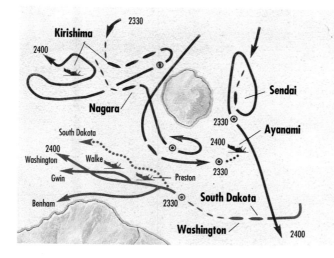

While the Japanese subjected the closer South Dakota *to intense punishment, the undetected* Washington *concentrated her fire on* Kirishima.

By this time most of her crew had been taken off by *Uranami*. The remainder, her captain and thirty others, abandoned ship just before she sank and made it by boat to Japanese-held shoreline. Meanwhile efforts to save *Kirishima* proved futile. Her crew was evacuated to three destroyers, taking with them the portrait of Emperor Hirohito that had hung in the officers' wardroom. Just before three-thirty, the second Japanese battleship to meet her end in Guadalcanal waters rolled over to starboard and swiftly sank.

The American battleships' guns had done their work. They had sunk an older and inferior Japanese battleship and a single enemy destroyer. In return Lee had lost two of his four destroyers, *Preston* and *Walke*, and a third, *Benham*, was mortally damaged. The status of his second battleship was unclear until 0215, when *South Dakota* finally repaired her damaged radio antennae and made contact. Lee was relieved to learn that her wounds were superficial and she would live to fight another day. Although Lee's victory was far from overwhelming, he had prevented the Japanese from bombarding Henderson Field. The fate of Admiral Tanaka's convoy would determine the battle's final score.

Tanaka, who had observed distant gun flashes from the battle around Savo, faced a difficult choice. He would reach the designated debarkation point off Tassafaronga (on the eastern side of Cape Esperance) just after dawn. Standard unloading procedures would expose his destroyers and the four remaining transports to daytime enemy air attacks. Reluctantly he concluded that he must either retreat or run the transports aground. This latter idea was rejected as too radical by Admiral Mikawa, now back in Rabaul, but Admiral Kondo, in direct command of Tanaka's operation, overrode Mikawa's objections.

Accordingly, just before dawn the four transports ran

up on the Tassafaronga beach and Tanaka's destroyers withdrew at top speed, still carrying on board many survivors from the ships that had sunk the day before. The troops on the beached transports made it safely ashore, but a good part of the provisions and precious medical supplies were destroyed by the fierce enemy air raids, and even fiercer bombardment from destroyer *Meade,* that came with daylight. (*Meade,* escorting a single cargo ship to Tulagi, only arrived on the scene that morning.)

F OR PHARMACIST'S MATE SECOND CLASS RAYMOND Kanoff and the other medical corpsmen aboard *South Dakota*, the battle really began when the firing stopped and the ship's public address system called all corpsmen to the tower foremast to attend to the wounded there. This was easier said than done. Ladders had been shot away, fires raged and torrents of water from firehoses poured down the superstructure. Kanoff waded through this knee-deep flood—it ran red with blood—to the base of an undamaged ladder, then worked his way as high up as he could, dressing wounds, applying tourniquets and administering morphine as needed. Occasionally men called out for their mothers or girlfriends. There was no screaming, but he did see two wounded friends crying in each other's arms. Some of the worst injuries were burns, the result of the scalding steam from the ruptured line to the ship's whistle. The most seriously wounded men were placed in canvas bags

(Above) Smoke rises from the burning Japanese transports beached near Cape Esperance near dawn on November 15. (Below) Ray Kanoff, a medical corpsman on South Dakota. *(Opposite top) Battle damage to* South Dakota. *(Opposite left) Members of the ship's company signal an*

overly optimistic battle tally for the action at the Santa Cruz Islands and the Naval Battle of Guadalcanal— twenty-three planes and three ships. (Opposite right) South Dakota's Captain Gatch, his arm still in a sling, leads a memorial service after the battle.

stiffened with wooden battens and lowered by ropes to the main deck. When he'd finally done what he could, Kanoff returned to the wardroom. There one of the ship's doctors was dealing with 150 wounded, aided by only a handful of corpsmen. So Kanoff pitched in.

At daylight he headed up the tower again; it seemed to be half shot away. Where a shell had pierced the radio direction finding room he could see clear through the superstructure. Since all the flag lines had been shot away, the Stars and Stripes flew from the signal bridge. Only now did the full magnitude of what had happened hit home.

As Gunner's Mate Charles Carpenter surveyed the ravaged superstructure, he wondered how on earth he had managed to come through without a scratch. Ensign Gerald Norton emerged from turret number one to discover that several fellow officers, with whom he'd eaten his last meal before the battle, had died. Chief Electrician's Mate James Bowen, who'd spent the

battle in the main battery plotting room, searched in vain for his brother John, a machinist's mate who'd been assigned to a repair party. After looking everywhere else, he finally found John snoozing in his bunk.

Thirty-nine men died on *South Dakota*, and fifty-nine were wounded. Most of these casualties occurred in the forward superstructure. The smell of death lingered for many weeks in these spaces, even though they were sprayed with formaldehyde. (Ray Kanoff, who spent another two and a half years on *South Dakota*, swears the odor never quite disappeared from some areas.) One survivor was the ship's mascot, a Boston terrier named Rascal. After the battle Captain Gatch found the dog in his emergency cabin just off the bridge. He was surrounded by wreckage and sound asleep.

The toll on the destroyers was far worse: 117 died on *Preston*, 80 on *Walke*. Most of the survivors from these two ships, many of them wounded, were picked up the following morning. *Benham*, whose spine was broken and bow missing, had left the battle area under her own steam, but was unable to navigate rising seas and was sunk by *Gwin* that afternoon. *Benham's* entire crew transferred safely onto Admiral Lee's last destroyer and made it safely back to port.

WHEN THE THREE-DAY NAVAL MARATHON ENDED, both sides claimed victory. If one includes those lost during the air raids on Tanaka's transports, total Japanese casualties were probably somewhat greater, but a simple count of ships sunk and men killed does not settle the score. The Japanese did not achieve their two essential aims. The Tokyo Express failed to make its biggest delivery in full and lost ten precious transport ships in the process. Far more important, Henderson Field survived, ensuring American air supremacy in the skies around Guadalcanal. Neither side yet knew it, but the beaching of Tanaka's transports marked the last major Japanese effort to reinforce the island.

More than twenty thousand Japanese troops remained on Guadalcanal, but they would soon be in grave danger of running out of the most basic essentials. In the second half of November, with the burgeoning Cactus Air Force making night destroyer runs ever more risky, submarines took over the Tokyo Express. But their limited capacity made them an inadequate alternative. (A supplementary scheme involving smaller surface craft quickly foundered.) As November drew to a close, the Japanese troops on the island were becoming desperate for food and medical supplies. One infantry commander noted in his diary that his entire nourishment for several days consisted of a single dried plum.

The Japanese were not so desperate, however, that they failed to put up fierce resistance as General Vandegrift moved to rekindle the land offensive temporarily abandoned before the mid-November sea battles and to exploit the lull in Japanese activity that followed their conclusion. In the second half of November his troops again advanced west of the Matanikau. But the Japanese lines held just west of Point Cruz, and there his troops would be stuck until well after Christmas. Clearly the Japanese were far from beaten, a fact underscored by the events of the night of November 30. This was the last important naval battle fought in Guadalcanal waters, the Battle of Tassafaronga.

The catalyst was a modest resupply convoy under

(Above) At the Battle of Tassafaronga on November 30th, a group of Japanese destroyers was surprised by a far superior force of American warships, yet defeated it soundly. (Right) The heavy cruiser Northampton *was one of four American ships torpedoed during the battle, although it was the only one to sink. (Far right) The stern of the heavy cruiser* Pensacola *clearly shows the scorch marks from fires started by an enemy torpedo during the battle.*

Admiral Tanaka. Submarines having proved woefully insufficient, the Japanese had improvised further, devising a system in which fast destroyers would race to Cape Esperance, pausing only long enough to drop drums filled with food and medical supplies offshore for pickup by small boats. Just before 11 P.M. on November 30, Tanaka arrived off Tassafaronga with the first of these deliveries—eight destroyers, laden with full supply

drums. His force was surprised by a far superior American force, consisting of four heavy cruisers, one light cruiser and six destroyers. The American commander, Rear Admiral Carleton Wright, was new on the scene, but he possessed a sound battle plan that included the intelligent deployment of ships with SG radars, and his force caught the Japanese in total disarray. Yet it was Tanaka who scored a decisive victory. All the American

torpedoes missed, Tanaka's destroyers quickly regrouped and devastated the enemy with their Long Lances, picking off four American cruisers "like mechanical ducks in a carnival shooting gallery," in the words of Samuel Eliot Morison. American gunfire managed to disable just one Japanese destroyer. When the brief battle was over, heavy cruisers *Pensacola*, *New Orleans*, *Minneapolis* and *Northampton* had all been ripped open by

Hit by two torpedoes, the bow of Minneapolis collapsed during the Battle of Tassafaronga. The cruiser limped to a sheltered harbor where a temporary bow could be fitted.

torpedoes. *Northampton* sank early the next morning; only Herculean feats of damage control saved the others.

Various reasons have been put forward for this debacle. American gunnery was certainly ineffective, a problem relating to the slow firing rate of the guns on the heavy cruisers and the high-speed maneuvering of the Japanese destroyers. More important, the American task force was a pickup team cobbled together in the aftermath of the mid-November naval battles, while Tanaka's ships fought in seasoned fighting units. Morison blamed the defeat on an American failure to give their destroyers adequate tactical independence. He noted that at the opening phase of the battle, before the American forces were detected, Admiral Wright refused to let his destroyers attack independently, thus denying them their best chance at an effective torpedo attack. But as Richard Frank points out, this critique overlooks more fundamental problems: "merely changing the formation could not cure underlying shortcomings in indoctrination and equipment." In other words the Japanese were still better at night fighting, despite the fact that the Americans held the technological trump card—radar. And Japanese

torpedoes were light years ahead of the American in both reliability and destructive power. However, damaging as it was to American naval pride, the Battle of Tassafaronga did nothing to alter the larger strategic balance.

In December both sides geared up for another Japanese attempt to retake the island. Belatedly the

(Above) A U.S. torpedo boat crew examines a Japanese submarine sunk trying to get supplies to troops on Guadalcanal.

Japanese began constructing an airstrip at Munda on the island of New Georgia, a mere 175 miles from Henderson Field. (How priceless this would have been back in August and September!) Despite the clever ruse of stringing palm fronds on wires to camouflage construction, the field was detected and soon became the target of daily bombing raids. Although the Munda airstrip was completed, it never became an effective base of air operations—and soon turned into a liability. Meanwhile more than fifty thousand Seventeenth Army troops gathered in Rabaul under Lieutenant General Hitoshi Imamura with orders to recapture Guadalcanal. The planned push would come early in the New Year.

But simply keeping the troops already on Guadalcanal alive was becoming more and more difficult. The Cactus Air Force was getting better at intercepting Tokyo Express runs, and the PT boat squadrons based at Tulagi were proving increasingly effective at night actions. On December 11, with a waxing moon making night operations more difficult to conceal, the last destroyer run of the year dropped supply drums off Tassafaronga. For the rest of the month the meager supply line would again be maintained by submarines, which meant the troops were left to suffer even more from starvation and disease. (Nighttime attempts to drop supplies from Betty bombers were quickly abandoned.)

The Japanese soldiers on Guadalcanal lived in increasingly desperate circumstances. Many were starving or wracked with disease, reducing the fighting strength of some units by as much as two-thirds. Those still relatively healthy watched more of their comrades die every day. Malnutrition left everyone in a weakened state. The men ate anything they could find—roots, coconuts, even grass. Various captured diaries hint at the horror of this situation. On December 26 one Japanese soldier confided to his journal, "We are about to welcome the New Year with no provisions; the sick are moaning within the dismal tents, and men are dying daily. We are in a completely miserable situation. . . . Why should we be subdued by these blue-eyed Americans? I intend to get onto the enemy airfield and let two or three of them have a taste of my sword. . . . O friendly planes! I beg that you come over soon and cheer us up!"

As the Japanese on the island grew weaker, the Americans grew stronger. Supplies and fresh army troops flowed in steadily. On December 9, an exhausted General Vandegrift was relieved by General Alexander Patch, and on the same day the first contingents of the First Marine Division, which had served on Guadalcanal since the initial landings in early August, left the island. Sailors were shocked by the condition of these tough veterans. Lieutenant Christian Merillat reported the scene: "On this occasion 'raggedy ass marines' was a fitting name for the weary, disease-ridden, bedraggled troops who filed into the landing craft and then hauled themselves, sometimes with difficulty, up the cargo nets to the decks of transports. They were dressed in frayed green dungarees or dirty khaki, stained with Cactus sweat and muck. Socks had become a luxury; many had long since rotted away. Boondockers were run down at the heels, tied up with knotted laces or bits of string. Almost

Emaciated prisoners of war provide grim evidence of the sad state of the Japanese forces as the Americans tightened their grip on the island.

everyone had lost many pounds. Hundreds had malaria." Some were too weak to climb the nets unaided and had to be lifted up. By early January the whole First Marine Division would be gone.

Come the New Year, with his forces both renewed and strengthened, General Patch was determined to drive the Japanese off Guadalcanal before they could return in even greater numbers. However the next great Japanese offensive was never to materialize. In early January, the Imperial Army finally accepted what the navy had been arguing for weeks: Guadalcanal was lost. In Tokyo, Prime Minister Tojo reluctantly ordered that the remaining troops be evacuated and that attention be turned once again to the bogged-down campaign on New Guinea. But Allied intelligence failed to catch

(Above) By January 1943, American land forces were pushing rapidly west along Guadalcanal's north coast. But when they arrived at Cape Esperance (below), only the hulks of beached transports remained to greet them.

even a hint of this sea change in military policy. And so, as the Japanese prepared to leave, the Americans commenced their biggest land offensive since arriving on the island, a coincidence that led to a something of an anticlimax to a long and bloody struggle. As the Japanese withdrew westward, the American troops advanced in the same direction. It was puzzling, but General Patch had to assume this retreat was tactical. Surely the enemy was regrouping for yet another big push. Such an interpretation was bolstered in late January by news of increasing naval activity at the Japaneses bases at Rabaul and Buin (at the south end of Bougainville), exactly the sort of activity that had preceded the big offensives in September and October. In reality, the Tokyo Express was about to run in reverse.

During the first seven days of February, nearly eleven thousand emaciated and sickly Japanese soldiers were ferried from the island on fast destroyers in three major nocturnal evacuations. Until the very end, the Americans believed that the destroyers were bringing in fresh troops, not taking them away. On February 8, the first American soldiers to walk on Cape Esperance beaches found them littered with abandoned boats and supplies. On February 9, General Patch concluded the Japanese were gone and sent this welcome message to Admiral Halsey: "Am happy to report this kind of compliance with your orders. . . 'Tokyo Express' no longer has terminus on Guadalcanal." It was almost exactly six months to the day since the First Marines' boots had crunched the gray sand of Beach Red.

RUINS OF EMPIRE

West of Savo Island lies
the sad wreck of the battleship *Kirishima*,
upside down in the mud. Her loss, together
with *Ayanami*, in the second part of the
Naval Battle of Guadalcanal, signaled the
turning point in Japanese attempts to drive
the Americans from Guadalcanal.

TWO JAPANESE SHIPS SANK DURING THE SECOND phase of the Naval Battle of Guadalcanal—the destroyer *Ayanami* and the *Kongo* class battleship *Kirishima*. We discovered *Ayanami* by accident as we were investigating a sonar target we expected to be either *Astoria* or *Vincennes*, two of the American cruisers sunk in the earlier Battle of Savo Island. The Japanese destroyer made a strange sight. Her stern sat upright but forward of the forecastle the bow had broken off and lay on its starboard side, as if a giant had twisted the ship. (In all likelihood the hull held together until it hit the

(Above) Our warship expert, Chuck Haberlein (right), watches images transmitted from the sea floor. (Below) Divers prepare Sea Cliff for a descent.

After Scorpio *has been lowered (top) a diver (above) photographs it below the surface. (Right)* Sea Cliff *in her hangar is prepared for a night launch. Problems with her batteries cut short our first dive on* Kirishima.

bottom, then broke at a point already weakened by the Japanese torpedoes that sank the destroyer after the crew had been evacuated.)

Kirishima was close to where she was supposed to be—only a mile from the spot west of Savo Island where Japanese navigators estimated she sank. But locating the battleship proved to be easier than photographing her. When *Sea Cliff* descended for our first dive on the wreck, we discovered that a strong current had whipped up the sediment, making maneuvering more difficult and visibility poor. We worried that we might get tangled up in the ship's ruined superstructure.

As we came in slowly on the port side near the bow, a wall of steel gradually materialized out of the particle fog. But something was wrong: the hull was upside down. Passing slowly along the keel, we discovered that the whole ship had turned over. The most abject image of all was the sight of her huge propellers and rudders

sticking up helplessly with the anchor chain wrapped around them. It was almost as if the great battleship was hiding its face in shame at its defeat.

A problem with one of *Sea Cliff*'s batteries forced us to resurface prematurely, but I had glimpsed enough to know that I had never seen a wreck like this. It may be that *Kirishima*'s unusually tall superstructure, a feature of Japanese battleships, prevented the ship from righting herself as she sank, as has every other ship I've found in deep water. Or there may be another explanation. *Kirishima*'s bow had broken off at a point approximately under her forward superstructure. The bent and ripped hull plates and the dense nearby debris field suggest a magazine explosion that probably happened after she left the surface. This may have prevented her from turning upright.

Of all the lost ships on the floor of Iron Bottom Sound, *Kirishima* is perhaps the saddest.

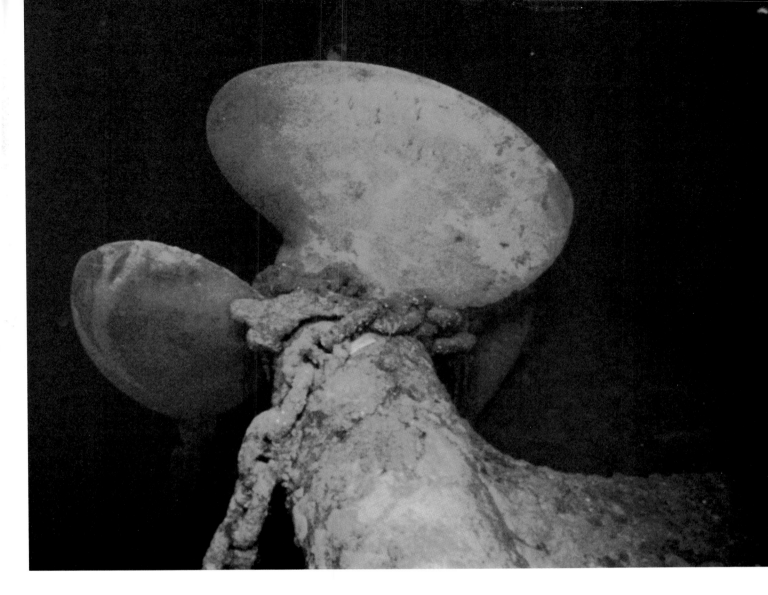

KIRISHIMA

BLOODIED IN ONE OF HISTORY'S LAST BATTLESHIP-TO-
BATTLESHIP ENCOUNTERS, *KIRISHIMA* WAS LEFT A
FLOATING WRECK, CIRCLING HELPLESSLY. TODAY SHE
LIES BROKEN AND UPENDED ON THE SEA FLOOR.

*(Above) One of
Kirishima's giant
propellers, now cinched
with the anchor chain.
(Below) The weight of the
Kirishima's towering*
*forward superstructure may
be the reason the ship failed
to right itself as it sank.
(Overleaf)* Kirishima *as
she looks today, her bow
and the tip of her stern gone.*

AYANAMI

SENT AHEAD ALONE ON THE NIGHT OF NOVEMBER 14, 1942, *AYANAMI* FELL UNDER THE GUNS OF THE BATTLESHIPS *SOUTH DAKOTA* AND *WASHINGTON*, WHICH LEFT HER BURNING AND HELPLESS.

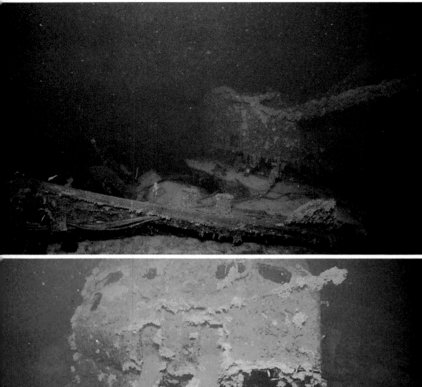

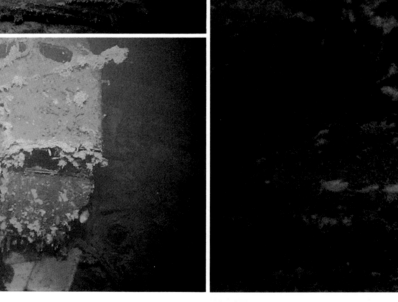

(Right) Ayanami *as she was. (Top) One of her stern turrets, battered and exposed. (Above)* Ayanami's *forward turret is now tipped sideways, along with the destroyer's shattered bow. (Above right) Gunfire and corrosion have combined to open up the side of the control center for one of* Ayanami's *torpedo batteries. The wheel was used to aim the Long Lance torpedoes (left).*

CHAPTER SEVEN

GUADALCANAL FAREWELL

August 14, 1992

I T WAS THE NIGHTS ON IRON BOTTOM SOUND THAT really got to me. By day its blue waters ringed by lush and mountainous tropical islands formed a scene difficult to reconcile with the stories of bloody warfare on land, in the air and at sea. True, the sun can be punishingly hot, but these days the heat is a plus, part of what makes Guadalcanal an increasingly popular resort for Australian tourists. And by day we were always busy diving on the wrecks we had found, battling currents, sediments and equipment failures— the usual travails of an underwater expedition. At night we would haul the submarine *Sea Cliff* and the submersible *Scorpio* back on board and embark on another sonar hunt for the ships we hoped to find. (In the end we managed to locate almost everything on our wish list and to represent each phase of the two big battles.) At night our vessel became quiet except for the throb of her engines, and there was time to think.

After each technicolor sunset, the surrounding islands quickly faded into the dark and a cool breeze sprang up, often wafting the scents of tropical flowers to us out over the water. It was possible then to imagine exhausted sailors who'd spent hours sealed belowdecks in armor-plated warships taking a brief turn topside

The wreckage of war off modern-day Guadalcanal.

A tropical sunset silhouettes our research ship, the Laney
Chouest. *(Inset) Bringing* Sea Cliff *on board for the night.*

before heading back to their battle stations; possible to
imagine other men sleeping fitfully at their gun mounts
or in the handling rooms or the radio rooms or at gun
directors—part of their minds ever alert to the chance
that on this night the enemy would be there.

With darkness, pinpoints of light could be seen on
Guadalcanal, but Savo, which is still sparsely populated
and lacks electricity, simply vanished into the gloom
until the moon rose. I remember a night when a finger-
nail moon gave the volcanic loom of Savo an especially
ghoulish feel. It was no longer a romantic, mystical Bali
Hai, but a sinister, foreboding place. Then I felt some

of the fear that the Japanese and American sailors must
have felt before a night battle. The most primitive
fear of all is fear of the dark. How much worse is it when
combined with fear of an invisible enemy?

Then I was able to imagine the blackness pierced by
a blinding green-white flare or glaring searchlight and
the silence shattered by the bleat of klaxons and the rau-
cous loudspeaker call to general quarters. And then the
brief, confusing battle like a crazed nightmare—the
roar and flash of gunfire, the express-train whoosh and
whistle of shells tracing red arcs against the night sky,
the sickening lurch of a torpedo hit followed by the
cries of the wounded, the engines stopping, the ship
drifting without power, aflame and sinking fast, men
clinging to empty powder drums or flotsam wreckage

in the tepid black saltwater, dogged by the fear of sharks, of the enemy's return, of what the morning would bring.

It was at night that the battles for Guadalcanal became real, stood out in stark contrast to our daylight contest of modern-day technology versus the elements. Nonetheless, as we explored the wrecks another sort of reality hit home to me. As with the *Bismarck*, I learned there is no substitute for seeing the literal evidence of war—shell holes in blasted metal, guns and torpedo tubes still trained as if to fire or pointing crazily askew, the wrecked bridge where a captain or an admiral breathed his last. The search for this reality was our real purpose in coming to Guadalcanal—to bring back images that would fill out the story in the history books, to mark and memorialize this great submarine

battlefield, to make dead ships live again.

It was an expedition different from any I have undertaken. For one thing, the sheer scale and scope of the search outweighed all my previous hunts for sunken ships. We explored more than 300 square miles of sea floor, an area greater than the combined search areas for the *Titanic* and *Bismarck*. We found the wrecks of thirteen ships, positively identifying twelve (the one we're uncertain about is either *Little* or *Gregory*, destroyers converted into fast transports that sank during a minor night action in early September 1942). We found the first ship fired on in the Battle of Savo Island, the Australian heavy cruiser *Canberra*. And we found the last big ship sunk by either side during the marathon Naval Battle of Guadalcanal, the battleship *Kirishima*. We

(cont'd on page 203)

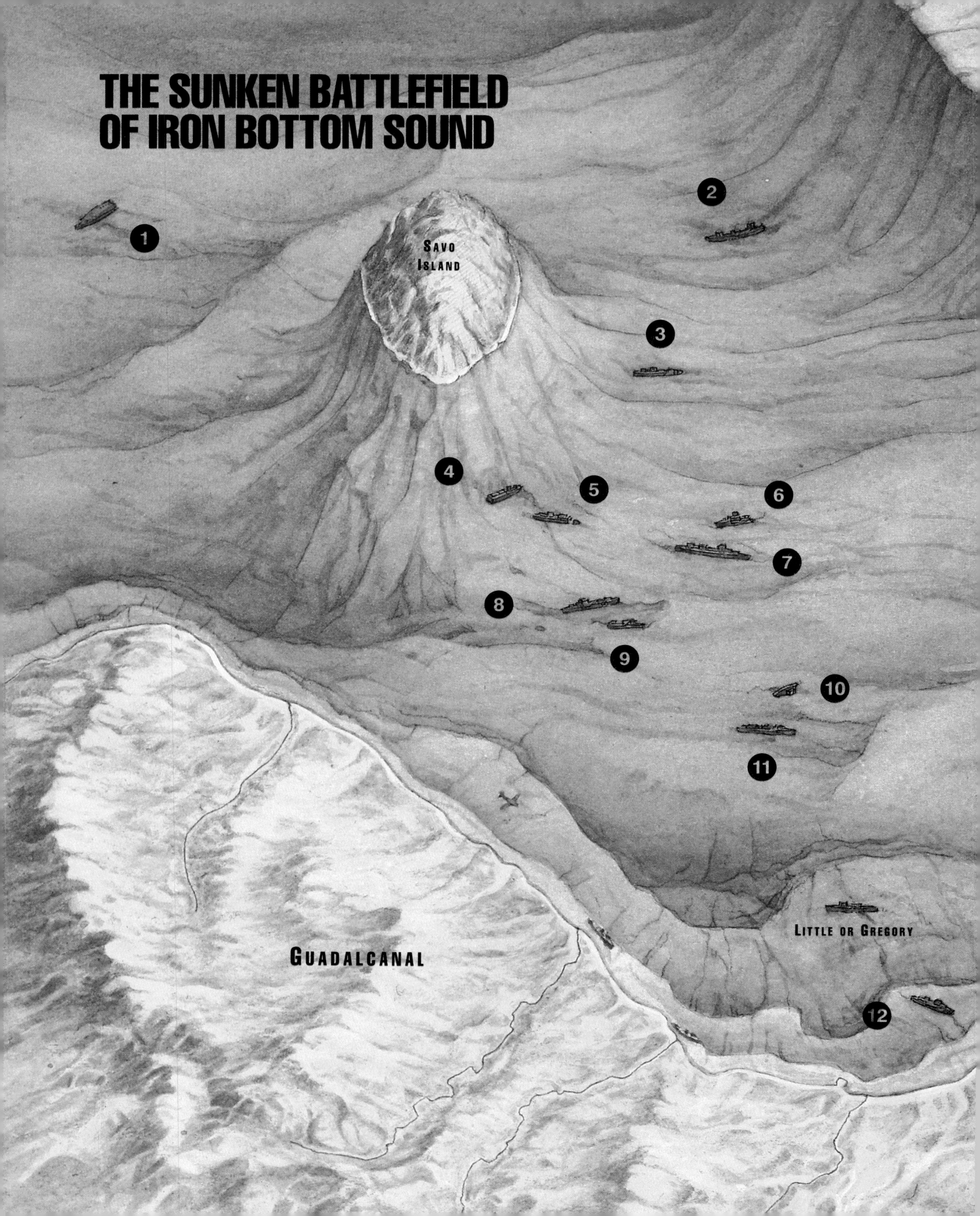

THE SUNKEN BATTLEFIELD
OF IRON BOTTOM SOUND

SAVO
ISLAND

1

2

3

4

5

6

7

8

9

10

11

12

LITTLE OR GREGORY

GUADALCANAL

In all, we discovered thirteen wrecks on the floor of Iron Bottom Sound, of the nearly fifty ships that make this one of the world's great submarine battlefields. This artist's rendering shows the approximate positions of the ships we found, as well as shallow-water relics of the fifty-year-old battle — wrecked transports and aircraft.

1.– KIRISHIMA

7.– CANBERRA

2.– QUINCY

8.– NORTHAMPTON

3.– AYANAMI

9.– CUSHING

4.– DeHAVEN

10.– BARTON

5.– YUDACHI

11.– MONSSEN

6.– LAFFEY

12.– ATLANTA

HENDERSON FIELD

The destroyer DeHaven, sunk by Japanese bombers on February 1, 1943, was the last American warship lost in the Guadalcanal campaign.

(Top) Her port propellers and (left and above) one of her guns today. (Below) DeHaven as she was, sailing in front of Savo Island.

found wrecks in remarkably good shape, given the beating they took, and wrecks blasted into pieces almost beyond recognition.

Many of the wrecks were not where we expected to find them. For example, *DeHaven*, sunk in early February 1943 when the fight for Guadalcanal was almost over, was a complete surprise. We weren't looking for her and we found her three miles from her reported sinking location. Such errors are hardly surprising. The heat of battle is not the time for navigators to be worrying about the exact spot where a ship has sunk. And there were some disappointments. We looked for, but did not find, Michiharu Shinya's ship, the *Akatsuki*, sunk in the early hours of November 13. It is conceivable, as Shinya himself pointed out, that the ship we identified as *Ayanami*, from the Japanese cursive A on her stern, is instead the vessel he served on. But both our historical consultants, Richard Frank and Charles Haberlein, remain convinced that this wreck's location is simply too far from the spot where *Akatsuki* is supposed to have sunk. (In the end, Shinya had to agree.)

Unlike our previous expeditions, at Guadalcanal we were fortunate to have survivors of the battles with us on board. This added an extra emotional dimension to the experience of confronting these ghosts from the past. And sometimes an ironic dimension as well. I was particularly struck by the contrast between the modern military men on board—the U.S. navy submarine officers—and the returning veterans of a distant war. The submariners were gung-ho boy scouts, excited about piloting their sub over sunken wrecks in a challenging and dangerous training mission. I suppose they were little different from the nineteen- and twenty-year-old sailors on both sides who in 1942 sailed into their first battle ignorant of war's reality.

Thank God these young, enthusiastic navy men have never experienced a real battle, have no memories like those of Bert Warne, Jim Cashman, Stewart Moredock and Michiharu Shinya. But despite the gulf between young and old, the generations got on famously. For example, as soon as the young submariners learned that Moredock had been an admiral's operations officer, they gave him the standard navy nickname, "Ops." Moredock at one point commented, "I love these guys. With them I think our future is in pretty good hands."

(Above) Four veterans meet aboard Laney Chouest (left to right): Roy Uyehata, U.S. Army veteran, Michiharu Shinya of Akatsuki, Bert Warne of Canberra and Stewart Moredock of Atlanta. (Left) Dr. James Cashman, wearing his Cushing association baseball cap. (Right) Bert Warne, Michiharu Shinya and Stewart Moredock pose in front of Sea Cliff.

The present-day technological battle was nothing compared to the battles these four men relived while on board. In this regard, one episode above all stands out for me. We had been trying in vain to get more than muddy pictures of Moredock's ship *Atlanta*, the only shallow-water wreck we explored. It is in roughly 300 feet of water and close to shore, a situation that made it tougher, not easier, to photograph. The tidal currents were too powerful and the sediments in the water too thick for us to get any really good pictures or video footage. This was frustrating for all of us, especially Moredock. We wanted him to be able to take another look at *Atlanta*'s bridge, perhaps even gaze on the spot where he saw Admiral Norman Scott take his last step.

I was myself in a gung-ho, boy scout frame of mind when I put on headphones to listen in on the interview that Robby Kenner, director of the National Geographic documentary about our expedition, was conducting that day with Moredock. Until that moment I had been preoccupied with the technological battle. When I tuned in to the interview, my mood quickly shifted.

Moredock talked about how his decision to return with us to Guadalcanal culminated a long period of coming to terms with his war experience. For most of the past fifty years he had pushed away any navy or Guadalcanal connection. When his children asked him what he did in the war, he fell silent. When one of his old shipmates tracked him down and invited him to a reunion, he politely demurred. When someone wanted to interview him for yet another book about some aspect of the Guadalcanal story, he refused. He led his life as a professor of mathematics at the University of Sacramento and tried to forget about November 1942.

Gradually, however, he noticed a transition in his attitude. And in the past few years some subterranean urge had brought him to confront this past. He'd even made a visit to Japan to stare his former enemy in the face—and found that face to be a human one. When he first arrived on board our ship, he met Michiharu Shinya, the torpedo officer on *Akatsuki*, which some credit with having fired the torpedo that knocked *Atlanta* out of the battle so early. Both of these men now hate war; they might even describe themselves as pacifists. While in prison camp in New Zealand, Shinya began to read the Bible. Eventually he converted to Christianity and ultimately he returned to Japan to become a minister in the United Church of Christ. But it was still hard for either

man to completely forgive and forget.

The ice between them melted pretty quickly. First Shinya told Moredock that as far as he knew, *Akatsuki* hadn't fired at all that night—certainly not torpedoes—so it wasn't his ship that crippled *Atlanta*. Then he complimented Moredock on *Atlanta*'s gunnery, which he credited with sinking *Akatsuki*. Not that it would really have mattered either way. As soon as they began to talk, they found they had much more in common than separated them. Men of the same generation who had fought in the same war and suffered greatly because of it. Soon they were asking about each other's lives. Do you have children? How is your wife? Next time you're in Japan/America you must come to visit me.

Now I listened as Moredock answered the interviewer's questions. Through him I began to relive that awful night. When he talked about the young guy on the next stretcher who turned and smiled so sweetly at him, then died, Moredock broke down and cried. And I found I had tears streaming down my cheeks as well.

Having survivors with us brought home much more piercingly the reality of wars and how they change the lives of those who fight them. In this book we have spent most of our time describing two great sea actions. But there is another, unwritten story of what happened to these men after the brief, cauterizing moment of battle. I'll always remember Moredock describing the long months of recuperation in a navy hospital. One foot and both of his hands and arms were in casts from all the shrapnel he'd taken. He could hardly do anything for himself and found the experience humiliating. Finally one arm had healed enough for the cast to be removed. The first thing he did was scratch his nose. "I'll never forget the relief of scratching that itch," he said. It was like reentering the human race.

You could write a whole book about what happened to these men after their battles were over. Here are a few snapshots. George Faulkner, the "debonair dustman" on *Canberra*, had just finished his watch in the engine room and hit his hammock when the Battle of Savo Island exploded. Faulkner survived without a scratch, but his best friend on board, Billy O'Rourke, was killed. When the crew returned to Sydney, Faulkner went to see Billy's girlfriend to give her the news. Three years later they were married. (Faulkner told me that on their last leave before *Canberra* sank, he and Billy got identical tattoos on their left forearms—a simple design consisting of a rose with the word "Mother." To this day, whenever he looks at the tattoo, he thinks of his dead friend.)

Another snapshot is of Bill Montgomery of *Quincy*. He was wounded during the battle and spent the night on a floating cork net with his head cradled in another seaman's lap. Montgomery recovered from his wounds and returned to active duty. Eventually the war took him to Oran in North Africa, where he repaired ships and prepared to take part in the invasion of Sicily as part of a beach-jumping battalion—logistical support that followed the initial amphibious landings. This time he was lucky. He became a star with the local navy basketball team and thus too valuable to morale to risk in the invasion. His team won the league championship and he was one of four members picked for the all-star team that represented the navy at the Allied games in North Africa.

Understandably, most of those whose ships sank during one of the night battles were happy to see the last of Guadalcanal. Most were shipped out immediately, but some were not so fortunate. After *Atlanta* sank on November 13, her junior gunnery officer, Lloyd Mustin, was assigned to the naval detachment on Guadalcanal, where he spent the next four months as operations and intelligence officer. *Atlanta* quartermaster George Petyo left the island physcially behind but not figuratively. Later in the war he found himself assigned to escort carrier *Lunga Point*, named after the point of land off which his ship was sunk.

For those with wounds as serious as Stewart Moredock's, the war was effectively over when their ships went down. But many others returned to participate in the ensuing battles of the Pacific campaign—Tarawa, Guam, Leyte Gulf, Iwo Jima, Okinawa, to name a few. Bert Warne's lungs were never the same after his escape through *Canberra*'s smoke-filled lower decks, but he went back to active duty, serving on sub chasers and air/sea rescue craft. After the war a few men stayed in the navy. Lloyd Mustin went on to command his own ships and eventually became an admiral.

(Above) Bert Warne and Stewart Moredock with one of the memorial plaques we placed on the wrecks. This one, laid on Canberra *by* Sea Cliff, *commemorates the ships lost in the Battle of Savo Island.*

So did Butch Parker, so briefly the captain of *Cushing*. But most returned to civilian life. *Cushing*'s Jim Cashman was one who succeeded in picking up where he had left off. He went back to his wife and his medical practice in Rawlins, Wyoming. He lives there still.

These are a few glimpses of those who survived. This book is equally a tribute to those who died. But as much as their stories, the memories I have brought away with me from Guadalcanal are images in my mind's eye: the wrecked ships lying on the floor of Iron Bottom Sound. Each of these lost ships died differently and each one presents a different mask of death, some of them uncannily apt. The long stern section of *Kirishima* lies upside down, like a Samurai warrior hiding his head in the humiliation of defeat. *Ayanami*, the little destroyer that suddenly found itself facing Admiral Lee's whole task force, is amazingly intact, although twisted out of shape, her stern section upright, her bow section lying on its side. *Canberra* is badly damaged but dignified, "still a lady," to quote Bert Warne who viewed her with us for the first time in fifty years. (Bert later commented that when he saw the lovely bouquet of soft coral and sea anemone that now graces A turret, it seemed to him as if *Canberra* had dressed ship for the occasion of our submarine visit.) The hundred-foot-long bow piece of destroyer *Barton* is the saddest image of all. She simply lay down on her side and died. *Quincy*, as befits the American ship the Japanese say put up the best fight at the Battle of Savo Island, is in many ways the best preserved and most spectacular wreck. Her bridge is still there, although the wings have collapsed and the rangefinder platform at the top front of the bridge structure is peeled up and back. She looks dangerous, still ready to fight on.

Quincy also gave me the most memorable underwater image of the entire expedition. On August 10, almost fifty years to the day after the ship sank, I was watching *Scorpio*'s remote transmissions as we made our first photography dive over *Quincy*'s wreck. As we came up in front of the bridge,

(cont'd on page 210)

The Iron Bottom Sound battlefield is impressive, but the island of Guadalcanal has its own reminders of war. (Top) This American Lightning fighter is now part of a village museum. (Above) A captured Japanese field piece and (below) a burned-out American tank, still sitting where it broke down.

It isn't just Guadalcanal itself or the depths of Iron Bottom Sound that still bear the scars of battle. The warm shallows off Guadalcanal contain their reminders, too. One is an American fighter (right) that ditched long ago. Another is the light cruiser Atlanta (below). A victim of the first part of the Naval Battle of Guadalcanal, the Atlanta now rests on her side in an underwater ravine (top and above).

Sea Cliff was positioned behind and off to one side so that its lights sent golden shafts radiating toward us from the bridge windows—an eerie image of the Rising Sun that sank her.

I've always been fascinated by battlefields on land, and I have walked on many American ones dating from the Revolutionary War and the War Between the States: Saratoga and Fort Ticonderoga; Gettysburg, Vicksburg and Bull Run, to name a few. I've been to Little Big Horn, where Custer made his famous last stand. When I explore these places I can visualize the battles, place my feet in the boots of the men who fought them.

A naval battlefield is different, especially one where multiple battles were fought. In one sense it is still as chaotic and confused as were the battles themselves. No one has turned the graveyard into a well-manicured park, or etched inscriptions on its gravestones. But it is a quiet and contemplative place.

Now that our expedition is over and this book is written, I can also walk in the shoes of the men who fought in Guadalcanal's treacherous waters. I can taste the salt and sun they tasted, feel the clench in their stomachs in the silence before the first salvo, hear their cheers when an enemy ship burst into flame or the deafening explosion when an enemy shell hit home.

James Michener, visiting Guadalcanal a few years after the war, wrote that "to me—and to many like me—Guadalcanal has a significance that is hard to explain." Specifically Michener was talking about how this "stinking" island became a proving ground for his generation, a place where young American soldiers and sailors dispelled the assumption—held by the Japanese

to their cost—that they'd grown too soft for war. Certainly one wonders if the nineteen- and twenty-year-olds of today would fare as well in her jungles and on her seas against an equally implacable foe. Perhaps. Perhaps not. But from this more distant point in time the pivotal events that began in early August 1942 take on a universal quality. Samuel Eliot Morison, dean of the American naval historians of World War II, came closest to the truth when he wrote, "For us who were there, or whose friends were there, Guadalcanal is not a name but an emotion." The whole range of human emotions, the whole spectrum of human strengths and weaknesses.

It seems appropriate to give the last words here to one of the men who fought at Guadalcanal, Stewart Moredock. "My decision to return to Guadalcanal wasn't a sudden thing, but a gradual transformation over many years. Even so, I hesitated about returning, afraid I'd get locked into a process that makes war into a game, that glorifies it, that would force me to masquerade as some kind of hero. I'm not a hero. I simply happened to be there. I was very reluctant to come back. But finally my family talked me into it. As one of my kids said to me, 'Dad, I think you're ready.'

"I remember standing at the Japanese monument at Mount Austen, a spot from which I could view the whole scene—Savo Island, Cape Esperance, Lunga Point, Henderson Field. It all seemed so small and insignificant, this place where so many battles were fought in the coal-black night. The Japanese monument is for all veterans on both sides, the inscription in both Japanese and English. Standing there, looking out over Iron Bottom Sound, I felt a sense of healing reconciliation."

(Left) Stewart Moredock visiting the American memorial overlooking the Matanikau River. For the fiftieth anniversary of Guadalcanal, a new American monument was dedicated at a ceremony to mark the campaign.

Veterans from many countries attended (above, top and middle right). Coastwatcher Martin Clemens (right) also returned to Guadalcanal for the fiftieth anniversary and is seen here greeting some of his surviving scouts.

AN ARTIST'S GUADALCANAL

War artist Dwight Shepler's images of battle.

Displayed throughout this book are a selection of works by the American war artist Dwight Shepler. A professional artist who specialized in sailing and skiing scenes, Shepler joined the navy after Pearl Harbor, thinking that he was putting painting aside for the duration. Instead, he became an official war artist, with orders to go where the action was and record it. Shepler joined Admiral Halsey's South Pacific fleet, and was aboard the American cruiser *San Juan* during the battle of the Santa Cruz Islands in October of 1942.

One month later, when the *San Juan* put in at Guadalcanal, Shepler decided to stay behind. During his few weeks on the island he recorded several key moments as the battle for Guadalcanal reached its climax. No pro-

Dwight Shepler (above right) at work on a Pacific invasion beach later in the war. (Right) Mass for the Fallen, *one of the works Shepler painted on Guadalcanal.*

pagandist, Shepler also captured scenes of day-to-day life. His straightforward, unposed watercolors accurately evoke the atmosphere of this dramatic chapter of the Pacific war.

Later in the war, Shepler witnessed the D-Day Invasion and the invasions of the Philippines and Okinawa. He stayed in the navy until 1947, and was ultimately promoted to commander. As a civilian, he continued to paint professionally until his death in 1972.

It is a gift to history that an artist as talented as Shepler captured the essence of that long-ago campaign in his vigorous watercolors.

Other works by Shepler can be seen on pages 8-9, 24-25, 94-95, 104-105, 162-163, 167, 169 and 182.

APPENDIX

Acknowledgments

It is impossible to thank all of the people in the United States Navy who helped to make this project a success, but we would like to give particular thanks to Admiral R.J. Kelly, Commander in Chief of the Pacific Fleet; Rear Admiral Henry C. McKinney, Commander of Submarine Force Pacific Fleet; Commodore Thomas J. Elliott, Jr., Commander of Submarine Development Group 1; and Commander Robert T. Appleby, Commander of the Deep Submergence Unit and his *Sea Cliff* Detachment and Unmanned Vehicle Detachment.

To me the most important people in any expedition are those who go to sea, take the risks, and overcome the problems that arise. And so, I want to thank Lieutenant Commander Christopher Raney for his ongoing support and dedication to this project and to the men he led during our two-year field program: the sonar search team in 1991 and the *Scorpio* and *Sea Cliff* teams as well as the officers that supported our 1992 expedition. Thanks also to the crews of the Australian R/V *Restless M* and the R/V *Laney Chouest* that served us so well for those two years.

I want to thank Jill Schoenherr of S.A.I.C. for her superb navigational skills and for providing the project with state-of-the-art navigational equipment and software to help us locate the lost ships of Iron Bottom Sound.

I also want to thank our team of engineers from the Marquest Group: Martin Bowen, Stu Harris and Emile Bergeron as well as David Mindell and Andy Bowen, who stood their watches and kept our imaging cameras rolling.

It is extremely difficult to work on the tangled remains of warships in the dark abyss let alone know their true identity. But thanks to the dedicated assistance of Richard Frank and Charles Haberlein, Jr., who accompanied us on our second voyage, we were able to unravel the story of each ship we wanted to tell. The final resting places of the warships that were lost during this historic battle are within the territorial waters of the Solomon Islands Government. I am very grateful for their cooperation and assistance in securing the necessary permits to carry out our research. In addition, I would like to thank Mr. Gerald Stenzel and his staff at TRADCO shipping for their unflagging logistics support and for managing to bridge a gap halfway around the world.

And most important, I want to thank my wife Barbara, who found herself, shortly after our marriage, tromping through the jungles of Guadalcanal, standing a navigation watch at 2 o'clock in the morning, watching me disappear beneath the waves in a submarine, and organizing this massive two-year effort.

Finally, we all want to thank the numerous veterans who lived through this historic series of events and then had to live through them again with us as we worked to retell their stories of those who were left behind.

Madison Press Books and Rick Archbold would like to thank the following for their contribution to the book.

Michiko Sakai Smart found many of the Japanese pictures, and Linda Goldman hunted down American photographs and arranged for the National Geographic Society to photograph material at the National Archives. Holly Reed at the National Archives and Record Administration also deserves special thanks, as do Charles Haberlein, Jr., and Edwin C. Finney, Jr., at the Naval Historical Center.

Alison Trinkl, of National Geographic Televison in California, helped us track down the many veterans we interviewed. Thanks also to Robby Kenner, the director of the National Geographic special on Guadalcanal, to Maya Laurinaitis, with National Geographic Television in Washington, and to Jill Shinefield, with National Geographic Television on the West Coast, who had copies made of many rare veterans' pictures.

Matthew Woodhead at the Australian War

Memorial and John C. Date of the Australian Naval Historical Society made sure that the Australian contribution to the campaign was adequately covered in pictures.

The following individuals helped either by agreeing to be interviewed, by providing crucial information, or by supplying us with many of their unique photographs...

Ted Blahnik and Harry R. Horsman of the Association of Guadalcanal Campaign Veterans;

Irvin H. Reynolds, of the Edson's Raiders Association;

Michiharu Shinya of *Akatsuki*;

Edward Corboy, Captain Henry K. Durham, David Driscoll, Stewart Moredock, Vice Admiral Lloyd Mustin and George Petyo, of U.S.S. *Atlanta*;

Percy Ackerman, George Faulkner, Henry Hall, Dr. Kenneth Morris, and Bert Warne of H.M.A.S. *Canberra*;

James Cashman, Donald Henning, E. William Johnson and Al McCloud of U.S.S. *Cushing*;

Bert Doughty, Joseph Hughes and Clyde Storey of U.S.S. *Monssen*;

Nathaniel Corwin, John Giardino, Harris Hammersmith, and Thomas Morris of U.S.S. *Quincy*;

Ray Kanoff and Charles Carpenter of U.S.S. *South Dakota*;

John A. Brown of U.S.S. *Washington*;

Mrs. Shirley Mesimer, widow of Grady F. Mesimer, and Mrs. Edward Parker, who provided us with pictures belonging to their late husbands.

Thanks also to Harry S. Grauberger for his photographs, and to Larry Weirs of the Sioux Falls, South Dakota, Public Works Department, who had the road to the U.S.S. *South Dakota* Battleship Memorial plowed after a snowfall so he could send us material on U.S.S. *South Dakota*, and to Martin Dowding, who compiled the index, and to Omar Lopez-Cruz of the University of Toronto Department of Astronomy.

Finally, a special thanks to Ralph Ingram, Jr., for lending us his as yet unpublished book on *South Dakota* as well as transcripts of interviews he conducted with former crew members of both *South Dakota* and *Washington*.

Photograph and Illustration Credits

Every effort has been made to attribute all material reproduced in this book correctly. If any errors have occurred we will be happy to correct them in future editions.

All underwater wreck pictures © Odyssey Corporation.

Front Cover: Painting by Ken Marschall.
1   Crest courtesy of Harry R. Horsman.
2-3   David Gaddis.
4-5   Bettmann Archive, U956972-INP.
8-9   *Lookouts on Bloody Knoll* by Dwight Shepler. Navy Art Collection, Naval Historical Center, #32.

CHAPTER ONE
10-11 Michael McCoy.
11   Michael McCoy.
12   Robert D. Ballard © Odyssey Corporation.

13   (Top) 20th Century Fox.
       (Bottom left) Toronto Public Library.
       (Bottom right) Toronto Public Library.
14-15 (Bottom) Michael McCoy.
14   (Top) Michael McCoy.
15   (Top) Bettmann Archive U960205-INP.
16   David Gaddis.
17   (Top) Harry S. Grauberger.
       (Bottom) Michael McCoy © National Geographic Society.
18   David Gaddis.
19   (Top) David Gaddis.
       (Center) Michael McCoy.
       (Bottom) Michael McCoy.
20   (Left) Naval Historical Center, NH 63438.
       (Right top) National Archives, 80-G-19930.
       (Right middle) *Mainichi* newspaper, Tokyo, Japan.
       (Right bottom) Popperfoto.
21   Map by Jack McMaster.

       (Left) Popperfoto.
       (Top right) Imperial War Museum, MYF 17584.
       (Bottom right) Imperial War Museum, MH 6492.
22-23 *Mainichi* newspaper, Tokyo, Japan.
22   Map by Jack McMaster. Australian War Memorial, 129750.
23   (Top left) *Mainichi* newspaper, Tokyo, Japan.
       (Top right) *Mainichi* newspaper, Tokyo, Japan.

CHAPTER TWO
24-25 *Tulagi Secured* by Dwight Shepler. Navy Art Collection, Naval Historical Center, #42.
26-27 National Archives, 80-GK-563.

101 United States Naval Institute.

102 National Archives, 80-G-17489, courtesy of Richard B. Frank. (Center) *Maru,* C-0801. (Bottom) Imperial War Museum, MH 5931.

103 *Mainichi* newspaper, Tokyo, Japan.

104-105 (Top) *The Ground Crew* by Dwight Shepler. Navy Art Collection, Naval Historical Center, #37. (Center) National Archives, 208-N-4932, courtesy of Richard B. Frank.

104 (Left) National Archives, 208-AA-75KK-11. (Center) Crest courtesy of Harry R. Horsman. (Bottom left) National Archives, 127-N-108572, courtesy of Richard B. Frank (Bottom right) National Archives, 80-G-54611.

105 (Bottom left) National Archives, courtesy of National Geographic Society. (Right) Bettmann Archive, U966408-INP.

106 National Archives, 208-AA-76FF-1.

107 (Top) National Archives, 80-G-30073. (Middle left) Ted Blahnik. (Middle right) Ted Blahnik. (Bottom) National Archives, 127-N-55326.

108-109 (Top) National Archives, 127-N-55325.

108 (Left) *A New Air Strip Being Laid Down* by Aaron Bohrod. U.S. Army Center of Military History, CC 98515. (Bottom) National Archives, 80-G-12379.

109 (Bottom) *Aftermath Guadalcanal* by Aaron Bohrod. U.S. Army Center of Military History, CC 87639. (Bottom right) United States Naval Institute.

110 National Archives, 111-SC-163978.

111 (Top) National Archives, 208-N-16980, courtesy of Richard B. Frank. (Bottom) *Mainichi* newspaper, Tokyo, Japan.

112 (Top) Michael McCoy. (Bottom left) National Archives, 80-G-16435. (Bottom right) Edson's Raiders Association.

113 (Top) Harry R. Horsman. (Bottom left) Edson's Raiders Association. (Bottom right) National Archives, 208-N-54181, courtesy of Richard B. Frank.

114 National Archives, 80-G-20823.

115 Naval Historical Center, NH 95449, courtesy of Richard B. Frank.

117 National Archives, 80-G-41286.

118-119 *Fantasma de Guerra* by John Lea. Naval Historical Center, NH 89605KN.

118 (Top) National Archives, 80-G-34822, courtesy of Richard B. Frank. (Bottom) National Archives, 80-G-176150, courtesy of Richard B. Frank.

119 (Bottom left) National Archives, 80-G-33947. (Bottom right) National Archives, 80-G-33948, courtesy of Richard B. Frank.

120-121 National Archives, 80-G-20700.

CHAPTER FIVE

122-123 *The Battle of Guadalcanal* by John Hamilton. United States Navy Memorial Foundation.

124 (Top far left) *Maru,* D-0103. (Center far left) Naval Historical Center, NH 51879. (Bottom far left) *Maru,* B-0201. (Far right) Michiharu Shinya.

125 (Top) National Archives, 80-G-11671. Photograph by Joseph H. Bailey, National Geographic Society. (Bottom) Naval Historical Center, NH 95450.

126 United States Naval Institute. (Top inset) National Archives, 19-N-31935. (Bottom inset) National Archives, 80-G-15836.

127 *Maru,* 00002.

128 Stewart Moredock.

130 Map by Jack McMaster.

131 *Maru,* D-0104.

133 (Left) William Johnson. (Center) Mrs. Edward Parker. (Right) Henry Durham.

134-135 Painting by Wes Lowe.

137 James Cashman.

138-139 Painting by Wes Lowe.

140-141 Teiji Nakamura.

140 Teiji Nakamura.

143 Bert Doughty.

144-145 Painting by Wes Lowe.

146-147 United States Naval Institute.

146 (Top) Bettmann Archive, UPI 633088.

147 (Top) Bettmann Archive, 637806 (Acme). (Bottom) Naval Historical Center, NH 65048.

GRAVEYARD OF THE DESTROYERS

148-149 Robert D. Ballard © Odyssey Corporation.

149 (Inset) John Livzey © National Geographic Society.

150 (Left) Robert D. Ballard © Odyssey Corporation.

151 Painting by Ken Marschall.

152-153 National Archives, 19-N-24725.

155 (Top) National Archives, 80-G-15836.

156 (Bottom) National Archives, 80-G-13609.

158-159 Painting by Ken Marschall.

158 (Top) *Maru,* D-0801. (Bottom) Teiji Nakamura.

161 (Inset) Teiji Nakamura.

CHAPTER SIX

162 *Night Action off Savo* by Dwight Shepler. Navy Art Collection, Naval Historical Center, #46.

163 U.S.S. *South Dakota* Battleship Memorial.

Bibliography

Churchill, Winston S., and the Editors of *Life*. *The Second World War*. Volume 2. New York: Time Incorporated, 1959.

Dull, Paul S., *A Battle History of the Imperial Japanese Navy, 1941-1945*. Annapolis, Maryland: Naval Institute Press, 1978.

Evans, Alun. *Royal Australian Navy*. Australians at War. North Sydney, New South Wales: Time-Life Books (Australia), 1988.

Ewing, Steve. *American Cruisers of World War II*. Missoula, Montana: Pictorial Histories Publishing, 1984.

Frank, Richard B. *Guadalcanal*. New York: Random House, 1990.

Friedman, Norman. *U.S. Cruisers: An Illustrated Design History*. Annapolis, Md.: Naval Institute Press, 1984.

Friedman, Norman. *U.S. Destroyers: An Illustrated Design History*. London: Arms and Armour Press, 1982.

Gill, G. Hermon. *Royal Australian Navy, 1939-1942*. Australia in the War of 1939-1945, Series II, Navy, Volume 1. Canberra: Australian War Memorial, 1957.

Gill, G. Hermon. *Royal Australian Navy, 1942-1945*. Australia in the War of 1939-1945, Series II, Navy, Volume 2. Canberra: Australian War Memorial, 1968.

Hamilton, John. *War at Sea*. Poole and New York: Blandford Press, 1986. Distributed in U.S. Sterling, 1986.

Hammel, Eric. *Guadalcanal: Decision at Sea, the Naval Battle of Guadalcanal, November, 13-15, 1942*. New York: Crown Publishers, 1988.

Hammel, Eric. *Guadalcanal: Starvation Island*. New York: Crown Publishers, 1987.

Hara, Captain Tameichi, with Fred Saito and Roger Pineau. *Japanese Destroyer Captain*. New York: Ballantine Books, 1961.

Hersey, John. *Into the Valley: A Skirmish of the Marines*. New York: Knopf, 1970.

Howarth, Stephen. *Morning Glory: A History of the Imperial Japanese Navy*. London: Hamish Hamilton, 1983.

Hoyt, Edwin P. *Guadalcanal*. New York: Stein and Day, 1982.

Lord, Walter. *Lonely Vigil: Coastwatchers of the Solomons*. New York: Viking, 1977.

Manchester, William. *Goodbye, Darkness: A Memoir of the Pacific War*. Boston: Little, Brown, 1980.

McCoy, Michael. *Guadalcanal: Fifty Years On*. Honiara, Solomon Islands: Solomon Islands Artists Cooperative, 1992.

Merrillat, Herbert Christian. *Guadalcanal Remembered*. New York: Dodd, Mead and Co., 1982.

Mesimer, Grady F., Jr. *The History of the U.S.S.* Quincy *(CA-39)*. Privately published.

Morison, Samuel Eliot. *The Struggle for Guadalcanal: August 1942-February 1943*. History of United States Naval Operations in World War II, Volume V. Boston: Little, Brown, 1966.

_____. *The Two Ocean War: A Short History of the United States Navy in the Second World War*. Boston: Little, Brown, 1963.

Musicant, Ivan. *Battleship at War: The Epic Story of U.S.S.* Washington. San Diego: Harcourt, Brace, Jovanovich, 1986.

Odgers, George. *The Royal Australian Navy: An Illustrated History*. Hornsby, NSW: Child and Henry, 1982.

Payne, Alan. *H.M.A.S.* Canberra. Garden Island, New South Wales: Naval Historical Society of Australia, 1991.

Shaw, Henry I., Jr., *First Offensive: The Marine Campaign for Guadalcanal*. Marines in World War II Commemorative Series. Marine Corps Historical Center: Washington, D.C., 1992.

Shepler, Dwight. *An Artist's Horizons*. Weston, Massachusetts: Fairfield House, 1973.

Shinya, Michiharu. *The Path from Guadalcanal*. Trans. by Eric Hardisty Thompson. Auckland, N.Z.: Outrigger Publishers, 1979.

Smith, Holland M., and Percy Finch. *Coral and Brass*. New York: Bantam Books, 1987.

Steinberg, Rafael, and the Editors of *Time-Life* Books. *Island Fighting*. Alexandria, Virginia: Time-Life Books, 1978.

Tregaskis, Richard. *Guadalcanal Diary*. New York: Random House, 1943.

Van der Vat, Dan. *The Pacific Campaign: World War II, the U.S.-Japanese Naval War, 1941-1945*. New York: Simon and Schuster, 1991.

Watts, Anthony. *Japanese Warships of World War II*. London: Ian Allan, 1967.

INDEX

I

Iceland, 169
Ichiki, Colonel Kiyono, 98, *98*, 99, 100, 101, 110, 150
Ikazuchi, 132
Ilu River, *see* Alligator Creek
Imamura, Lt. General Hitoshi, 183
Inazuma, 132
India, 21
Ingram, Ralph Jr., 168
Into the Valley, (book)
Iron Bottom Sound, discovered wrecks in, map of, *200-201*; origin of name of, 12, 69; mentioned, *17*, 18, 69, 71, 72, 92, 97, 103, 114, 115, 120, 125, 127, 128, 142, 143, 144, 156, 164, 168, 169, 188, 197, 206, 207, 208, 211
Iwo Jima (Pacific battle), 206

J

Janeczko, Seaman Second Class Thaddeus, 66
Japanese, conditions for on Gauadalcanal, 183; numbers of, 180, 183
Japanese Combined Fleet, 101, 103, 119, 120, 143
Japanese Eighth Fleet, 28, 40, 101, 164
Jarvis, 42, 67
Java Sea, Battle of the, 20, 128
Jenkins, Warrant Radio Electrician Kenneth, 169

Jenkins, Captain Samuel, 128, 130, 131, 134, 142, 145, 146, 147
Jintsu, 102, 103
Johnson, Electrician's Mate First Class, William, 132-133, 137, 139, 140
Juneau, 127, 130, 138, 141, *146-147*, 150; sinking of, 147

K

Kabashima (sailor), *161*
Kako, 55, 68, *69*
Kanoff, Pharmacist's Mate Second Class Raymond, 178-179; photo of, 178
Kate (bomber), 164
Kavieng (New Ireland Is.), 68
Kawaguchi, Maj. General Kiyo-taki, 110, 111, 112, 113, 114
Kearney (New Jersey), 146
Kennedy, John F., *33*
Kenner, Robby, 205
Kieta (Bougainville Is.), 40
Kikkawa, Captain Kiyoshi, *140*, 141, 142
Kimura, Admiral Susumu, 171, 173
King, Admiral Ernest J., 14, 16, 69, 114
Kinryu Maru, 103
Kinugasa, 55, 57, 68, 116

Kirishima, condition of as wreck, 186-188, *189-191*, 206; damage sustained during battle, 176-177; location of, 188, 190- 191, *200*; sinking of, 177; mentioned, 123, *124*, 125, 130, 133, 137, 139, 164, 171, *174-175*,199, *201*
Koli Point (Guadalcanal Is.), 120
Kondo, Vice Admiral Nobutake, 164, 165, 168, *168*, 170, 171, 173, 176, 177
Kongo, 117
Kongo class (ships) 123, 168
Koreans, 45
Koro (Fiji Islands), 37
Kukum (Guadalcanal Is.), 145
Kyusyu Maru, *117*

L

Laffey, condition of as wreck, *156-157*; location of, *200*; mentioned, 126, 132, 138, 143, 150, *201*
Laney Chouest, 71, 72, *74-75*, *198-199*, *204*
Latta, Chief Quartermaster Rob Roy, 136, 146
Leckie, Private Robert, 40
Lee, Rear Admiral Willis Augustus, battle plan of, 168; character of, 165; mentioned, 164, *165*, 169, 171, 172, 173, 177, 180, 206
Leyte Gulf (Pacific battle), 206
Lightning (fighter), 207
Little, 199
Little Big Horn, 210

San Cristobal, 22; location on map, 22

San Diego (Calif.), 12

San Francisco, deaths aboard, 125; shells *Atlanta*, 134, 136; mentioned, *115*, 116, *125*, 126, 127, 130, 134, 138

San Juan, 46, 47

Santa Cruz Islands, Battle of the, 118, *118-119*, 119, 120, 140, 163, 165, 169

Santa Isabella Island, 49; location on map, *22*

Santa Isabella

Saratoga (U. S. Civil War site), 210

Saratoga, 26, 34, 101

Sasai, Lieutenant Junichi, 28

Sato, Captain Torajiro, 97

Savage, Bert "Doc" (ship's cook), 132

Savo Island; on map, *47, 130*; mentioned, 12, 17, 19, 27, 34, 46, 49, 50, 52, 60, 66, 69, 71, 115, 127, 138, 139, 142, *163*, 168, 169, 171, 173, 176, 177, 186, 188, 198, 203, 211

Savo Island, Battle of; date of, 16; U. S. defeated at, 16; mentioned, 16, 72, 74, 76, 114, 116, 164, 199

Schwitters, Petty Officer Merlin "Doc," 66

Scorpio, 18, 71, 72, *73*, 74, *151*, *188*, 197, 206

Scott, Rear Admiral Norman; Cape Esperance, victory for, 116, 117, 126; death of, 134; mentioned, 19, 46, *114*, 115, 127, 128, 130, 138, 164, 168, 205

Sea Cliff, 18, 71, 72, 74, *74-75*, *149, 151, 158-159, 187*, 188, *188*, 197, *198, 204*, 206

Selfridge, 66

Sendai, 171, 173, 176

Shakespeare, William, 32, 33

sharks, 16, 63, 65, 66, 142, 144

shells, piercing ability of, 168

Shepler, Dwight, 25, 94, 169

Shikanami, 176

Shinya, Lieutenant Michiharu, capture of, 146; during battle, 130-131, 132, 137-138; POW, 19, 205; mentioned, 123, *124*, 203, *204*, 205

Shokaku, 102, *118*, 119

Shortland Island, 28

Shortland Islands, 147, 164, 165

Sicily (Italy), 206

Singapore, 20, 48

Smith, Lieutenant Paul, 146

Smith, Lt. Commander Stewart, 145

SOC (scout biplane), 41

Solomon Islands, 12, 16, 19, 22, 30, 32

South Dakota, casualties on, 179; conditions on during battle, 178-179; mentioned, 120, 121, 163, 164, *164*, 165, *166*, 168, 169, 171, 172, 173, 176, 177, 178, *179*, 192

South Pacific, (musical), 11

Southard, 49

Southerland, Lieutenant James J. "Pug," 34

Spain, 22

Spam, 107

Spanish-American War, 27, 36

Spurgeon, Gunner's Mate Second Class Leo, 143, 144

St. George, Able Seaman Stephen, 50, 64

St. George's Channel, 39

Sterett, 126, 131, 138

Stokes, Commander T. Murray, 129, 137

Storey, Bosun's Mate Second Class Clyde, 143, 144

Strobel, Chief Bosun's Mate George, 61

Stutt, Sergeant William, 41

submarines, 125, 147, 180, 183, 203

Sullivan, Albert, *147*

Sullivan, Francis, *147*

Sullivan, George, *147*

Sullivan, Joseph, *147*

Sullivan, Madison, *147*

Sullivan, Signalman Third Class, 61

Sullivans, The, 147

"surrender ticket," 107

Suzuki, Captain Masakane, 132

Sydney (Australia), 31, 205

T

Tainan Air Group, 28

Taivu Point, 97, 111

Takama, Rear Admiral Tamotsu, 125

Takao, 171, 176

Takasuka, Commander Osamu, 130-131, 132

Tanaka, Rear Admiral Raizo, attacks Henderson Field, 117; mentioned, 97, 98, 101, *101*, 102, 103, 143, 147, 164, 165, 173, 177, 178, 180, 181, 182

Tanambogo Island, 30

Tarawa (Pacific battle), 206

Tassafaronga, Battle of, 180, *180-181*, 182

Tassafaronga (Guadalcanal Is.), 177, 178

TBS (Talk Between Ships), 128, 129, 130, 136

Tenryu, 55, 67

Thin Red Line, The (book) *13*

Titanic, 18, 72, 199

Tojo, Prime Minister, 184

Tokyo, 14, 118, 184

Tokyo Express, 103, 110, 114, 115, 116, 117, 121, 147, 180, 183, 185

Tongatabu, 165

torpedoes, *see* Long Lance, Mark XV

Tregaskis, Richard, 39, 98

Truesdell, Lt. Commander William, 57

Truk Island, 120, 123

Tulagi Island, 22, 25, 28, 30, 31, 36, 37, 39, 40, 42, 45, 49, 69, 98, 114, 171, 178; on map, *47*

Turner, Rear Admiral Richmond Kelly, complacency of, 49; ship losses of, 67; mentioned, 26, 37, 41, *41*, 45, 46, *46*, 47, 48, 66, 67, 69, 114, 115, 117, 124, 126

U

Uehlinger, Commander Archibald, 176

United Church of Christ, 205

Uranami, 173, 177

Uyehata, Roy, *204*

V

Val (dive bomber), 35

Vandegrift, Major General A. Archer, mentioned, 27, *36*, 37, *38*, 39, 45, 46, *46*, 49, 67, 96, 97, 98, 110, 111, 117, 120, 121, 171, 180, 183

Vicksburg (U. S. Civil War site), 210

"Victory at Sea," (TV series), 12

Vila (Efate Is.), 32

Vincennes, sinking of, 60, 63; survivors of, 65; sinking of, 60, 63; survivors of, 65; mentioned, 46, 47, 49, 55, 56, *56*, 57, *61*

Vouza, Jacob, *96*

Vunakanau Airfield (New Britain), 28

W

Walke, 171, 177; casualties on, 179

Walker, Commander Frank, 55

Walsh, Commander J. A., 64

Warne, Ordinary Seaman Albert, *Canberra* survivor, 19, 72; during battle, 54-55; mentioned, *54*, 203, *204*, 206

Washington (D. C.), 72, 114

Washington, 121, *163*, 164, 165, 168, 169, *169*, 171, 172-173, *174-175*, 176, 177, 192

Wasp, 102

Wellington, New Zealand, 79

Wildcat (fighter), *31*, 34, 35, 42, 97, 105

Wilson, 46

World War I, 32, 37, 66, 111, 124

World War II, 11

Wright, Rear Admiral Carleton, 181, 182

Wulff, Lt. Commander John, 147

Y

Yamamoto, Admiral Isoroku, 68, 103, 143, 168

Yamato, 121

Yoshiie, Kurato, 48, 49, 68

Young, Captain Cassin, 134, 136

Yubari, 55, *58-59*

Yudachi, condition of as wreck, 150, *158-161*; location of, *200*; sinking of, 143; mentioned, 127, 129, 139, *140-141*, 141, 142, *201*

Yukikaze, 143

Yunagi, 55

Z

Zero (fighter), 28, *29*, 30, 34, 35, 124

Zuiho, 120

Zuikaku, 102, 120